LANGUAGE ARTS 607
Stories

LIFEPAC Test is located in the center of the booklet. Please remove before starting the unit.

Author:
Della Johnson, M.A.Ed.

Editor-in-Chief:
Richard W. Wheeler, M.A.Ed.

Editor:
Elizabeth Loeks Bouman

Consulting Editor:
Rudolph Moore, Ph.D.

Revision Editor:
Alan Christopherson, M.S.

MEDIA CREDITS:
Page 7: © Photosdisk, Thinkstock; **25:** © karandaev, iStock, Thinkstock; **32:** © Photos.com, Thinkstock; **43:** © prawit_simmatun, iStock, Thinkstock.

804 N. 2nd Ave. E.
Rock Rapids, IA 51246-1759

Stories

Introduction

If we speak, listen, read, or write, our main purpose should be to share ideas. Time is wasted if we read and do not remember what we have read. We should read purposefully and wisely.

Words are important. Once a student told his teacher that he didn't like to read books. "You don't like books?" the teacher replied in surprise.

"I like books," the boy answered. "It's just the words I don't like."

If words trouble us, we should take time to get acquainted with them, to learn what they mean and to add them to our vocabulary. Words build vocabularies, and people who are successful usually have large vocabularies. The dictionary is a wonderful tool to help you. Use it. Build your vocabulary regularly.

Objectives

Read these objectives. The objectives tell you what you should be able to do when you have successfully completed this LIFEPAC. Each section will list according to the numbers below what objectives will be met in that section. When you have finished this LIFEPAC, you should be able to:

1. Give a definition of a true story.

2. Tell the main details of each reading selection in this LIFEPAC.

3. Arrange the events of each story in this LIFEPAC in the correct order.

4. Identify the clues that indicate the validity of a story or statement.

5. Show the relationship between cause and effect.

6. Identify the author's purpose or the main idea of a passage.

7. Spell words with the digraph *ea*.

8. Spell certain multisyllable words from the Bible.

9. Spell words with the *ear* letter pattern.

10. Spell certain number words.

11. Use nouns and pronouns correctly in a sentence.

12. Identify the adjectives in a sentence.

13. Identify some suffixes and tell what they mean.

14. Use demonstrative pronouns correctly in written sentences.

15. Write a business letter.

Survey the LIFEPAC. Ask yourself some questions about this study and write your questions here.

1. SECTION ONE

In this section you will study some skills that will help you read with greater understanding. You will study some ways you can help yourself learn to spell new words and add them to your Word Book. Also, you will study some writing rules and practice your writing skills.

Section Objectives

Review these objectives. When you have completed this section, you should be able to:

1. Give a definition of a true story.
2. Tell the main details of each reading selection in this LIFEPAC.
3. Arrange the events of each story in this LIFEPAC in the correct order.
4. Identify the clues that indicate the validity of a story or statement.
5. Show the relationship between cause and effect.
6. Identify the author's purpose or the main idea of a passage.
7. Spell words with the digraph *ea*.
8. Spell certain multisyllable words from the Bible.

Vocabulary

Study these words to enhance your learning success in this section.

agate (ag it). A kind of quartz stone with variously colored stripes, cloudy colors, or moss-like formations.

arid (ar id). Having very little rainfall; very dry.

austere (ô stir). Stern; very strict with children.

defy (di fī). To set oneself openly against someone or some authority.

drone (drōn). A male honeybee that does not work; an idler; a loafer.

eddy (ed ē). A small whirlpool of water.

exuberance (eg zü bur uns). The fact or condition of being overflowing with growth and health.

lure (lùr). To lead away by arousing desire.

stubborn (stub urn). Fixed in purpose or opinion.

tantalizingly (tan tu lī zing le). Teasingly with something desired in sight, but out of reach.

taunt (tônt). To jeer at; insulting remarks.

validity (vu lid u tē). Truth or soundness.

Note: *All vocabulary words in this LIFEPAC appear in* **boldface** *print the first time they are used. If you are unsure of the meaning when you are reading, study the definitions given.*

Pronunciation Key: hat, āge, cãre, fär; let, ēqual, tėrm; it, īce; hot, ōpen, ôrder; oil; out; cup, pùt, rüle; child; long; thin; /ᵮH/ for then; /zh/ for measure; /u/ or /ə/ represents /a/ in about, /e/ in taken, /i/ in pencil, /o/ in lemon, and /u/ in circus.

STORY—"LET GEORGE DO IT!"

"Let George Do It" is a true story. In the early 1900s George Warner became a much-loved missionary in China. Later he became president of a missionary organization with mission fields around the world. The events surrounding this story are told as his daughter and grandchildren remember them.

Often God uses little experiences in our childhood to help build character traits that make us what we are as adults. George Warner learned an important lesson and never forgot it.

George grew to be a man who served God in a responsible way, but he had been an irresponsible boy. Because each of us is sometimes irresponsible, we can feel as George felt. Being able to relate to the story gives the story human interest.

Disclaimer: In this story, the author uses the word 'Indian' to refer to the Native Americans and their land. Today, we typically use the specific names of the Native American Nations, or we use the term Native American. This has changed over time, and the author and characters did not intend to show any disrespect.

Let George Do It!
Della Johnson

1 Tall, lanky George walked barefoot along a dusty path in Alderdale, Washington. The **arid** country dazzled in the sunshine of a beautiful day. George's thoughts turned to the order Papa had just given him.

2 "George, I want you to help dig irrigation ditches today."

3 "What an unpleasant task!" thought George. Surely it was in his home the idea, "Let George do it," originated. The **taunts** of the boys now rang in his ears. They often chanted, "It was 18 and 65, George Segundus was then alive, a lazy old **drone** from the land of ..." George's thoughts continued to plague him. "Oh, why did my family call me George, and why do I have to work on a day like this? There are so many better things to do!" he thought.

4 Just then George spotted William, his older and only brother, at the bottom of the river bank. William was with a neighbor boy preparing the boat for a ride. "George, come with us for a ride," the boys called.

5 The sun sparkled **tantalizingly** on the waters of the Columbia River. The river always held a special **lure** for these adventuresome boys. The **exuberance** of youth filled George—his father's request was forgotten. George cupped his hands and yelled, "Here I come, wait." Running, he kicked at the sagebrush that would **defy** his advance.

6 George reached the boys and with one quick jump leaped into the boat. The boys paddled away. The breeze behind them licked the waters, bobbed the boat, and helped push them on their way. Little **eddies** swirled in the blue mass around them. The boys knew these waters well enough to avoid most of the contrary currents. The boys had become rather intimately acquainted with these **stubborn** pools from past experiences.

7 George looked toward the shore and saw the large sand dunes. What great fun they had rolling down these huge mounds of sand. In the summer warm winds would shift the sand and sometimes reveal treasures such as Indian arrowheads. Old timers said that long ago this area was an Indian burial ground.

8 Now the boys were passing an island in the middle of the river. Because of the many beautiful **agates** they found there, the Warner family had dubbed it Agate Island. Sometimes the family would take a boat and paddle out and have picnics on the island. There young imaginations could run wild. At one end of that island was an Indian burial ground. Papa carefully warned the children not to go near it. He reminded them that they must respect their Indian friends.

9 The day sped on; the boys took turns rowing the boat. It was a special thrill to feel strength flowing through their muscles as they won the battle against the tough currents of the mighty Columbia.

10 The sun warmed their bodies. George relaxed and looked at his brother. William was so strong and quiet. George laughed to himself as he thought of times not too long ago when he wondered if he, "the baby" of the family, would ever be strong enough to "get on top" in one of those brotherly squirmishes. That day had come. Now, once in awhile, he could compete and occasionally come out ahead.

11 The hours sped by quickly and the boys were now returning home. George looked up. The schoolhouse stood out more graphically than the other buildings of Alderdale. George chuckled to himself as he recalled an incident of only last week.

12 A group of young children had been sitting on the recitation bench. George had glanced up just in time to see something that roused his already strongly developed sense of humor. A stray cat had come in and had taken a seat between two of the children. All that could be seen of the cat were his ears over the top of the back of the bench and a swinging tail brushing back and forth between the back and seat of the wooden bench. Although usually a diligent, serious student, George had all he could do to control his laughter.

13 The skies were still blue, but a heavy cloud began to engulf George as he saw Papa coming slowly down the path. A strange feeling developed in his stomach. Now George realized what he had done. How would he face Papa? George's sensitive conscience was already hurting. In all the glory of this day, he had left a job undone and disobeyed his father. What would Papa do?

14 Papa was an impressive looking, dignified person with a balancing sense of humor. But Papa could be stern, and Papa expected obedience.

15 As they pulled up to the river bank, **austere** lines darkened Papa's face. Papa's voice was husky as he looked George in the eye. "George, do you want to be like this always?"

16 George hung his head, "No, Papa." Not another word was spoken as the two slowly made their way home. George vowed in his heart never to be so irresponsible again. He was thoroughly ashamed of what he had done. Through the years, his father's words were to ring in his ears many times.

Note: The town of Alderdale now lies quiet and still beneath the waters of the lake formed by John Day Dam.

Circle the correct answer for each question.

1.1 What mistake did George make?
a. He laughed.
b. He was ashamed of what he had done.
c. He disobeyed Papa.

1.2 What decision did George make?
a. Never to go boating again.
b. Never to be so irresponsible again.
c. Never to have fun again.

1.3 What did Papa's words mean?
a. George would never learn to dig ditches.
b. George shouldn't have fun.
c. George would be irresponsible.

Complete this activity.

1.4 Place an X before each word or words that accurately describes something found in this story.

a. _____ suspense

b. _____ humor

c. _____ human interest

d. _____ information

e. _____ mystery

Look for these words in the story "Let George Do It!"

1.5 In Paragraph one find a word that means *without shoes*. _____

1.6 In Paragraph one find a word that means *sparkled brightly*. _____

1.7 In Paragraph three find a word that means *started at a certain point*. _____

1.8 In Paragraph five find a word that means *to resist*. _____

1.9 In Paragraph eight find a word that means *named*. _____

1.10 In Paragraph twelve find a word that means *industrious*. _____

1.11 In Paragraph thirteen find a word that means *to cover or swallow up*. _____

1.12 In Paragraph sixteen find a word that means *promised or pledged*. _____

WORD BANK

arid	impressive
arrowheads	irresponsible
adventuresome	recitation
dignified	sensitive

Select a word from the Word Bank to complete each sentence.

1.13 The _____ country dazzled in the sunshine of a beautiful day!

1.14 The river always held a special lure for these _____ boys.

1.15 In the summer warm winds would shift the sand and sometimes reveal treasures such as

_____ .

1.16 A group of young children were sitting on a _____ bench.

1.17 George's already _____ conscience was hurting.

1.18 Papa was an a. _____ looking, b. _____ person.

1.19 George vowed in his heart never to be so _____ again.

READING SKILLS

Three reading skills will make you enjoy stories more. These three skills are called sequence, validity, and cause and effect. These skills will also help to make studying more profitable.

Sequence. The first skill is remembering the sequence, or order, in which events happened in a story. This skill will also help you remember the order of events in Bible study or social studies.

Place these events from "Let George Do It!" in the correct sequence.

1.20 _____ George reached the boys, and with one quick jump, leaped into the boat.

1.21 _____ "George, do you want to be like this always?"

1.22 _____ They were now approaching home.

1.23 _____ Tall, lanky George walked along the dusty path in Alderdale, Washington.

1.24 _____ George looked toward the shore and saw the large sand dunes.

1.25 _____ "George, come with us for a ride," the boys called.

1.26 _____ A strange feeling developed in his stomach.

Validity. A true story or a chapter from history often has within itself proofs of its validity. These proofs are to be found by certain tests. Does the author say the story is true? If the author says it is true, are dates, place-names, or other pieces of information given that may be checked in other sources?

Complete this activity.

1.27 Place an **X** in front of each statement that indicates the story is true.

a. _____ The author tells you George Warner was a real person.

b. _____ A stray cat had come in and joined the group.

c. _____ The breeze behind them licked the waters.

d. _____ The Columbia River borders Washington state.

e. _____ A date is given.

f. _____ The hours sped by.

Cause and Effect. Frequently the cause of something is stated immediately before the effect. Occasionally cause and effect are separated in the story. If they are, part of the fun of reading is thinking back to see if you can remember what caused events to happen as they did.

 Match the cause with the correct effect.

1.28 _____ William and friend

1.29 _____ breeze

1.30 _____ sand dunes

1.31 _____ agates

1.32 _____ sun

1.33 _____ cat on recitation bench

1.34 _____ Papa's simple words

a. offered great fun

b. made George forget his father's order

c. warmed their bodies

d. caused the boat to bob

e. encouraged the Warners to name the island *Agate Island*

f. caused George to make a lifetime decision

g. imaginations

h. made George chuckle

SPELLING AND HANDWRITING

You will review how to study words to learn to spell them correctly. You will also review some handwriting rules.

HOW TO STUDY A WORD

1. THINK   Pronounce the word correctly.
   Know its meaning.
   See if there are any unusual spellings of its sounds.
   Look for silent letters or double letters. Notice word endings.
   Look for sound patterns.

2. SOUND SYLLABLES
   Break the word into syllables.
   Say the word by syllables.
   Spell the word by syllables.

Spelling. When you study each of the spelling lists in this LIFEPAC, remember these four rules. Following this pattern when you study will help you.

3. LOOK   Look at the word as a whole.
   Now close your eyes and try to remember what it looks like.
   Now spell it to yourself.

4. REMEMBER
   Spell the word to yourself several times. Write the word until you know it.

SPELLING WORDS-1

already	forsaken	merciful	seat
arrowheads	great	patiently	transgressors
break	iniquity	prospereth	treasures
consume	irrigation	reach	unpleasant
envious	leaped	screamed	

When *e* and *a* are together, the *e* usually is long /ē/ as in *meat* or *seat*. Sometimes the *e* is short /e/ as in *bread* and *ready*, and sometimes it sounds like *a* as in *break* /ā/. The vowels *ea* are working together to make one sound. Vowels working together to make one sound are called a vowel digraph.

Look at the vowels in each word. Look for the *ea* vowel pattern.

 Complete this spelling activity.

1.35 Find ten words in Spelling Words-1 with the vowel digraph *ea*. The first one is done for you.

alr ea dy

a. _____   b. _____

c. _____   d. _____

e. _____   f. _____

g. _____   h. _____

i. _____

The digraph *ea* has three sounds. Look at these words. Each word is spelled phonetically. Say the word to yourself.

s ea t - sēt   h ea d - hed   br ea k - brāk

Complete the following activities.

1.36 Place each of the *ea* words from Spelling Words -1 under the word with the same sound.

seat	head	break
a. _____	a. _____	a. _____
b. _____	b. _____	
c. _____	c. _____	
	d. _____	

1.37 Read in your Bible Psalm 37. Locate eight words from Spelling Words-1 and write them after the verses in which they are found.

a. Psalm 37:1 _____

b. Psalm 37:1 _____

c. Psalm 37:7 _____

d. Psalm 37:7 _____

e. Psalm 37:20 _____

f. Psalm 37:25 _____

g. Psalm 37:26 _____

h. Psalm 37:38 _____

1.38 Write each word from Spelling Words-1 that is found in this Psalm. Be careful to use your very best handwriting. Write a definition for each word in your own words.

a. _____

b. _____

c. _____

d. _____

e. _____

f. _____

g. _____

h. _____

1.39 Do the following three things with each of the eight spelling words given. Use a dictionary if necessary.

Write the number of vowels in the ○.

Write the number of vowel sounds you hear in the □ .

Write the number of syllables in the △ .

a. consume ○ □ △   e. merciful ○ □ △

b. break ○ □ △   f. patiently ○ □ △

c. iniquity ○ □ △   g. prospereth ○ □ △

d. forsaken ○ □ △   h. transgressors ○ □ △

1.40 Find two spelling words in which the letters *ti* sound like *sh*.

Example: mention (men shun)

a. _____

b. _____

1.41 Find three words from Spelling Words-1 that are plural.

a. _____   b. _____   c. _____

1.42 Find the endings for these words.

a. envi _____   e. prosper _____

b. forsak _____   f. scream _____

c. merci _____   g. transgress _____

d. patient _____

1.43 Find three words that contain double consonants.

a. _____   b. _____

c. _____

ABC   **Ask your teacher to give you a practice spelling test of Spelling Words-1.** Restudy the words you missed.

Handwriting. Your handwriting gives an impression of you. Neat handwriting leaves a good impression. Work hard to write neatly!

1. Do you cross *t* and *x* ?
   Do you finish each word?

   t   x

2. Do all your letters touch the line?

   touch   the

   line

3. Do you round your letters?

   round   your

   letters

4. Does each new word (if not capitalized) begin with a stroke on the line?

   start   each

5. Do you finish your a and o correctly?

   word   on   the   line

   and   one

Do the following practice review on the cursive alphabet.

1.44 Look at these lowercase letters carefully and then follow the guide with your pencil.

a b c d e f g

h i j k l m n

o p q r s t u

v w x y z

1.45 Write each lowercase letter.

_____

_____

_____

_____

_____

_____

_____

_____

_____

_____

_____

_____

_____

A B C D E F G

H I J K L M N

O P Q R S T U

V W X Y Z

1.46 Study the models above. Write each capital letter. Be sure your letters touch the line.

1.47 Practice writing these letters. Be sure your capital letters slant correctly and touch the lines.

_D_

_P_

1.48 Practice these letters. These letters have a loop below the line. Be sure your _g_ does not look like _q_.

_f_

_g_

1.49 Write this verse in your very best handwriting. Look at the sample carefully. Follow the rules you have learned.

Depart from evil and do good. Psalm 37:27

TEACHER CHECK _____ _____
　　　　　　　　　　　　　initials　　　date

Review the material in this section in preparation for the Self Test. This Self Test will check your mastery of this particular section. The items missed on this Self Test will indicate specific areas where restudy is needed for mastery.

SELF TEST 1

Answer true or false (each answer, 2 points).

1.01 _____ In the early 1900s George Warner became a much-loved missionary in China.

1.02 _____ You always hear all vowel sounds in words.

1.03 _____ Papa didn't want George to have fun.

1.04 _____ The idea, "Let George Do It," originated in the Warner home.

1.05 _____ It is helpful to follow a pattern when you study.

1.06 _____ George could not remember what his father wanted him to do.

1.07 _____ When two vowels work together to make one sound, it is called a vowel digraph.

1.08 _____ If we speak, listen, read, or write, the main purpose should be to share ideas.

1.09 _____ It has been proved that successful people do not need large vocabularies.

1.010 _____ Every effect has a cause.

1.011 _____ Events placed in the order in which they happened are in sequential order.

1.012 _____ The Warners called the island *Agate Island* because they found so many agates there.

1.013 _____ Papa could be stern, and Papa expected obedience.

1.014 _____ The vowel combination *ea* is called a vowel digraph.

1.015 _____ The town of Alderdale now lies quiet and still beneath the waters of the lake formed by John Day Dam.

Write the correct word on the blank to complete each sentence (each numbered answer, 3 points).

1.016 Words build our _____ .

1.017 You should read _____ .

1.018 History or true stories usually contain evidence of _____ .

1.019 "Let George Do It!" is a _____ story.

1.020 The events surrounding this story are told as George's a. _____ and

b. _____ remember them.

1.021 Often God uses little experiences in our childhood to help build _____ traits.

1.022 The digraph ea can have _____ different sounds.

1.023 A group of young children were sitting on the _____ bench.

1.024 Old timers said that long ago the sand dunes had been an _____ ground.

1.025 When two vowels work together to make one sound it is called a vowel _____ .

Write a word from the Word Bank to correctly complete each sentence (each answer, 2 points).

┌─────────────────────── **WORD BANK** ───────────────────────┐

ashamed	irrigation	schoolhouse
dazzled	licked	stray
defy	mounds	swirled
engulf	pattern	syllables
experiences	plague	thrill

└──┘

1.026 The arid country _____ in the sunshine of a beautiful day.

1.027 "George, I want you to dig _____ ditches today."

1.028 George's thoughts continued to _____ him.

1.029 Running, he kicked at the sagebrush that would _____ his advance.

1.030 The breeze behind him _____ the waters.

1.031 Little eddies _____ in the blue mass around them.

1.032 What great fun they had rolling down these huge _____ of sand.

1.033 When studying spelling words, breaking the words into _____ is helpful.

1.034 It was a special _____ to feel strength flowing through their muscles.

1.035 Follow a _____ when you study.

1.036 The _____ stood out more graphically than the other buildings.

1.037 The boys had become rather intimately acquainted with these stubborn pools from past _____ .

1.038 A _____ cat had come in and joined the group.

1.039 A heavy cloud began to _____ George.

1.040 George was _____ of what he had done.

Answer each item in complete sentences (each answer, 5 points).

1.041 In your own words explain why it is important to have a good vocabulary.

_____

_____

1.042 Explain the lesson George learned.

_____

_____

_____

80/100   SCORE _____   TEACHER _____ _____
                                              initials   date

ABC **Take your spelling test of Spelling Words-1.**

2. SECTION TWO

In this section you will practice more skills to improve your reading comprehension. You will also find and mark nouns and pronouns in sentences. You will learn the skill of understanding word groups. You will learn to spell more words from the Bible and to spell a group of words with a letter-group pattern. You will continue to practice writing capital letters.

Section Objectives

Review these objectives. When you have completed this section, you should be able to:

2. Tell the main details of each reading selection in this LIFEPAC.

3. Arrange the events of each story in this LIFEPAC in the correct order.

4. Identify the clues that indicate the validity of a story or statement.

6. Identify the author's purpose or the main idea of a passage.

8. Spell certain multisyllable words from the Bible.

9. Spell words with the ear letter pattern.

11. Use nouns and pronouns correctly in a sentence.

Vocabulary

Study these words to enhance your learning success in this section.

consequently (kon su kwent lē). As a result; therefore.

corporal (kôr pur ul). The lowest noncommissioned army officer, next below a sergeant. He usually commands a squad.

glimmer (glim ur). A faint, unsteady light.

inexpensive (in ik spen siv). Not expensive; cheap; low-priced.

profusely (pru fyüs lē). Abundantly; freely.

providentially (prov u den shul lē). Proceeding from divine power.

reassuring (rē u shúr ing). Comforting; encouraging.

suburbs (sub urb). Town or village near a large city.

Pronunciation Key: hat, āge, cãre, fär; let, ēqual, tėrm; it, īce; hot, ōpen, ôrder; oil; out; cup, pút, rüle; child; long; thin; /ŦH/ for **then**; /zh/ for measure; /u/ or /ə/ represents /a/ in about, /e/ in taken, /i/ in pencil, /o/ in lemon, and /u/ in circus.

STORY—"MIDNIGHT CALLERS"

Read this story purposefully and notice details. China has been closed to missions for many years. In the early 1900s the door was open to missions even though war lords and bandits were making life difficult and dangerous for everyone.

The land of China was troubled and often missionaries were confronted with evil men or robbers. These greedy men sought anything of value. Many times the Lord wonderfully protected the missionaries. Often the missionaries kept **inexpensive** watches on hand to appease the robbers. They called these cheap watches "robber watches."

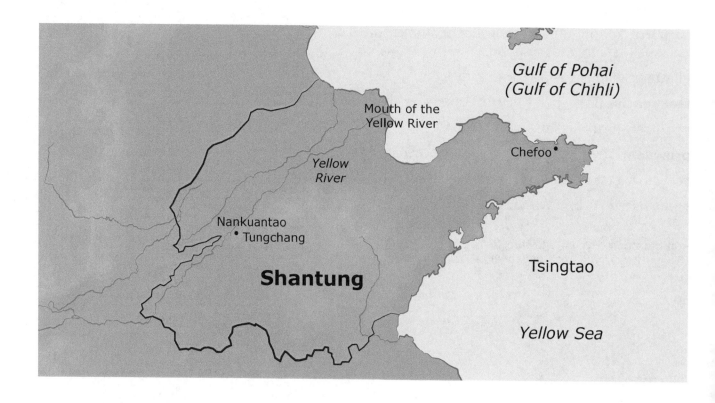

MIDNIGHT CALLERS
by Della Johnson

All was quiet in the mission station on the plains of Shantung Province (shan tung) in the great land of China.

The missionaries, Mr. and Mrs. Warner, had settled down for the night when they heard tap...tap... tap...on the window.

Quickly Missionary Warner sprang to his feet. He called, "Who's there?"

Immediately the familiar voice of the gateman replied, "Mr. Warner, open the door!" The voice was familiar, but the manner in which he spoke was strange. Could it be someone was telling him what to say?

As Missionary Warner left the room to open the outside door in the adjoining room, he turned to his wife and in **reassuring** tones said, "Don't be afraid!"

There were reasons for the missionary mother to be afraid. Rumors for several days had said that political conditions were at "sevens and eights." "Sevens and eights" is what the Chinese say when we would say "sixes and sevens," which refers to a state of disorder or confusion. Then too, the voice of the gateman sounded so strange at such an early hour in the morning! Here in the trundle bed beside Mamma baby Wilma lay sound asleep.

The outside door was opened. Immediately a masked face appeared, and a gruff voice announced, "I am going on a long journey and have come to borrow money. Unlock the screen door! Let me in!"

The bandit put meaning to his words by bringing out a gun and shaking it back and forth. A new missionary in China always learned quickly to obey orders, especially when the orders were given by bandits.

Having opened the screen door, Missionary Warner turned to go back into the bedroom. He immediately felt the sharp end of the gun that had been shaken in his face. Now it was roughly shoved against his back between his shoulders.

Providentially the batteries in the flashlight were badly in need of replacing. **Consequently**, only the object upon which the flashlight was directly focused could be seen. Mamma and baby went unnoticed. Baby Wilma continued to sleep.

Missionary Warner led the bandit to the small sack of Chinese dollars. "Get the money— quick!" the bandit ordered as he took the flashlight out of Missionary Warner's hand. The robber's whole body was shaking as if he were terribly afraid. Missionary Warner reached to the top of the wardrobe and took down the leather bag of silver dollars. The robber dropped the flashlight to grab for the money like a drowning man grabbing for a life line. With his gun in one hand and the flashlight on the floor, he could not see to take the money. Carelessly he laid his gun down.

As quick as lightning, something seemed to whisper to Missionary Warner, "Here's your chance! Knock him down, grab his gun. Be master of this situation." But Missionary Warner remembered that at least two more bandits were outside. At the smallest sign of commotion in the house, they would kill the night watchman, "Fien Feng," and all the missionaries would be in danger.

Missionary Warner gave the robber some clocks and watches. Now the bandit seemed satisfied. Loot in hand, he followed Missionary Warner to the living room. The moments were tense. In spite of the tenseness, Missionary Warner did not forget the Chinese courtesy due to any guest within the walls of his home.

In true Chinese fashion, Missionary Warner bowed low to his "new friend" and said in his best Chinese, "Will you please be seated while I make you a cup of hot tea?" This act of friendliness brought the **glimmer** of a smile to the bandit's face. He greedily clutched his loot and backed toward the door.

As the bandit stepped out of the door, he remembered his courtesy. He bowed and said, "Goodbye," which, in Chinese, is "I'll see you again."

As soon as the visitor departed, both missionaries knelt in prayer and thanked the Lord for His special care and deliverance from those wicked men. The total loss was not more than fifty dollars in gold.

The robbers became more and more bold in the **suburbs**. Missionary Warner prayed for a special verse of Scripture. The Lord gave him the verse in Daniel 4:25, "...The most High ruleth in the kingdom of men, and giveth it to whomsoever He will."

The missionaries realized that God was their protector, and no one could harm them unless God saw fit to let them do so.

Look for clues of the validity of the story.

2.1 In the first paragraph the author stated that his story took place in China. Place an **X** before each statement that verifies that idea.

a. _____ Political conditions were at "seven and eights," as the Chinese say.

b. _____ Could it be someone was telling him what to say?

c. _____ A new missionary in China always learned quickly to obey orders.

d. _____ The batteries in the flashlight were badly in need of replacing.

e. _____ Missionary Warner led the bandit to the small sack of Chinese dollars.

f. _____ Carelessly he laid his gun down.

g. _____ Missionary Warner did not forget his Chinese courtesy.

h. _____ Missionary Warner gave the robber some clocks and watches.

i. _____ In true Chinese fashion, Missionary Warner bowed low to his "new friend."

Circle the correct answer to complete each sentence.

2.2 In the first two paragraphs, the author is trying to
a. create suspense.
b. explain why the story was written.
c. set the scene and introduce the main characters.

2.3 This story is
a. sad.
b. exciting.
c. fictitious.

2.4 Missionary Warner was
a. a coward.
b. selfish.
c. courageous.

2.5 Missionary Mama was
a. sick.
b. frightened.
c. calm.

2.6 Baby Wilma was
a. sleeping.
b. crying.
c. sick.

Number these events in the order in which they happened.

2.7 _____ A masked face appeared and said, "I am going on a long journey and have come to borrow money."

2.8 _____ Mr. and Mrs. Warner had settled down for the night.

2.9 _____ The bandit said, "Goodbye," which in Chinese is, "I'll see you again."

2.10 _____ Tap...tap...on the window.

2.11 _____ Missionary Warner led the bandit to a small sack of Chinese dollars.

2.12 _____ Both missionaries knelt and thanked the Lord for His special care.

Complete each sentence with the correct word or words.

2.13 All was quiet in the mission station on the plains of a. _____ in the great land of b. _____ .

2.14 Rumors for several days had said that political conditions were at

a. "_____ and b. _____ ."

2.15 In the _____ bed beside Mamma baby Wilma lay asleep.

2.16 Providentially, the _____ in the flashlight were badly in need of replacing.

2.17 Mamma and baby went _____ .

2.18 At the least sign of a. _____ in the house, the bandits would kill the

b. _____ watchman.

2.19 Missionary Warner gave the robber some a. _____ and

b. _____ .

2.20 Missionary Warner _____ low to his "new friend."

2.21 The total loss was not more than _____ in gold.

2.22 The Lord gave Missionary Warner the verse in _____ .

GRAMMAR SKILLS

If you could have only two kinds of words with which to communicate, what would you choose? Probably *nouns* and *verbs*. The basic structure of language depends on these two kinds of words. Nouns are sometimes replaced by pronouns, which substitute for nouns. You will study and practice using nouns and pronouns correctly.

Nouns. What you need to know about nouns in order to use them correctly is in the following chart.

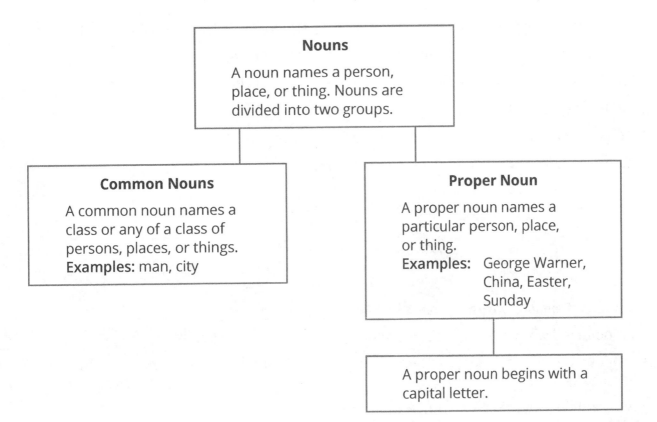

Nouns

A noun names a person, place, or thing. Nouns are divided into two groups.

Common Nouns

A common noun names a class or any of a class of persons, places, or things.
Examples: man, city

Proper Noun

A proper noun names a particular person, place, or thing.
Examples: George Warner, China, Easter, Sunday

A proper noun begins with a capital letter.

Find the nouns. Underline each common noun. Circle each proper noun.

Example: The land of China was troubled, and often missionaries were confronted with evil men or robbers.

2.23 These greedy men sought anything of value.

2.24 All was quiet in the mission station on the plains of Shantung Province in the great land of China.

2.25 The voice was familiar, but the manner in which he spoke was strange.

2.26 In the trundle bed beside Mamma baby Wilma lay sound asleep.

2.27 The bandit put meaning to his words by bringing out a gun and shaking it back and forth.

2.28 The batteries in the flashlight were badly in need of replacing.

2.29 The robber's whole body was shaking as if he were terribly afraid.

2.30 The robber grabbed for the money.

2.31 Missionary Warner gave the robber some clocks and watches.

2.32 The total loss was not more than fifty dollars.

Pronouns. *Pronouns are used in place of nouns.*

A pronoun is a word used in place of a noun.

A pronoun can replace a subject noun:
I, he, she, we, they.

A pronoun can replace an object noun:
me, him, her, us, them.

A pronoun can replace a possessive noun:
mine, his, her, their.

All of these pronouns are called personal pronouns.

Nouns

Example: *Mr.* and *Mrs. Warner* had settled down for the night.

Pronoun

Example: *They* had settled down for the night.

Find the pronouns. In the sentences draw a line under each personal pronoun.

Example: The story about Mr. and Mrs. Warner tells <u>their</u> experiences as missionaries.

2.33 Quickly Missionary Warner sprang to his feet.

2.34 The voice was familiar, but the manner in which he spoke was strange.

2.35 Missionary Warner turned to his wife and said, "Don't be afraid."

2.36 The bandit put meaning to his words.

2.37 He immediately felt the sharp end of the gun which had been flashed in his face.

2.38 The gun was roughly shoved between his shoulders against his back.

2.39 He had his gun in one hand.

2.40 He greedily clutched his loot and backed toward the door.

2.41 They knelt in prayer and thanked God for His special care.

2.42 Missionary Warner realized that God would not allow anyone to harm them against His will.

Write how you feel.

2.43 Would you have liked to live in China in 1900? Tell why or why not. Underline nouns and circle pronouns in your writing.

_____

_____

_____

_____

_____

_____

_____

_____

_____

_____

TEACHER CHECK _____ _____
                    initials   date

READING SKILLS

Every time you read a passage, you should look for the main idea. You need to practice this skill continuously. This skill is a basic study habit. After finding the main idea, you must note the details. One way to master the details of a passage is to understand word groups.

Main idea. Read the following story that has often been told about George Washington. Look for the main idea.

During the Revolutionary War, George Washington was a general and the commander-in-chief. His soldiers loved and respected him.

One very cold morning Washington went out to inspect a camp which was to be fortified. He wore a long cape and a hood that half hid his face. Nobody recognized him because his coat and uniform were covered.

Washington came upon a group of soldiers building a wall of logs. The **corporal** was busy giving orders. "Up with it now! Give it all your might!" he shouted. The men lifted the log and strained and pulled as hard as they could, but they simply could not raise it high enough.

Once again the corporal shouted to the men, but he offered them no help.

The men struggled, and just as the log was about to sink back, Washington stepped over to them. Washington was strong and helped them put the log on top.

The soldiers thanked the stranger **profusely**, but the corporal ignored him.

Washington turned to the corporal and sternly told him he should have helped his men.

"Is that so?" answered the man. "Can't you see that I am a corporal?"

Washington threw back his cape showing his uniform. "Well sir, I am your commander-in-chief! Won't you send for me the next time a log is too heavy for your men to lift?" Then Washington turned and walked briskly away.

Complete these activities on finding the main idea. Write the letter of the phrase that correctly completes the statement.

2.44 The best title for this story would be _____ .
    a. "Building a Log Wall"
    b. "The Commander-in-Chief"
    c. "An Act of Kindness"

2.45 The main idea of this story is that _____ .
    a. George Washington was general.
    b. The men were lifting logs.
    c. George Washington was kind.

Underline the common nouns once and proper nouns twice. Remember nouns name a person, place, or thing.

2.46 During the Revolutionary War, George Washington was general and commander-in-chief.

2.47 George Washington wore a long cape and hood that half hid his face.

2.48 The soldiers were building a wall of logs.

2.49 The corporal was busy giving orders.

2.50 Washington was strong and helped them put the log on top.

2.51 The soldiers thanked the stranger.

2.52 Washington threw back his cape showing his uniform.

2.53 Washington turned and walked away briskly.

2.54 No person is too important to offer an act of kindness.

Answer the following questions in your own words.

2.55 If you were one of the soldiers Washington helped, how would you feel?

_____

_____

2.56 If you were the corporal, how would you feel after George Washington talked to you?

_____

2.57 If you were George Washington, how would you feel when you saw the corporal refuse to help his men?

_____

_____

Understanding word groups. Everyone wants to share thoughts in a way that the reader or hearer will understand. To be sure people understand you, you must learn to say exactly what you mean. Words are grouped together to answer questions like "Who?" "What?" "Where?" "Why?" "How many?" and "How often?" Learning to find these word groups in sentences will help you remember the details of what you read. This skill will also help you to write and say exactly what you mean.

 Look at the words in italics. What question do they answer? Circle the answer.

2.58 George Washington was a *general and the commander-in-chief.*

    a. who   b. what   c. where

2.59 Washington went out to *inspect a camp.*

    a. who   b. what   c. where

2.60 Washington wore *a long cape and hood.*

    a. who   b. what   c. where

2.61 Washington *was strong and helped them.*

    a. who   b. what   c. where

2.62 The soldiers *thanked the stranger profusely.*

    a. who   b. what   c. where

2.63 Washington said, *"I am your commander-in-chief."*

    a. who   b. what   c. where

SPELLING AND HANDWRITING

Psalm 24 has words in it that are in Spelling Words-2. Other words are in the *ear* spelling pattern. Handwriting practice is on more capital letters.

Spelling. Review the study rules for learning spelling. Eleven of the words have the *ear* spelling pattern, but they are pronounced with three different */ear/* sounds.

SPELLING WORDS-2

ascend	deceitfully	fear	searched
bear	everlasting	generation	tear
commotion	earn	hear	vanity
consequently	early	learn	wear
dear	established	righteousness	year

LANGUAGE ARTS 607

LIFEPAC TEST

NAME _____

DATE _____

SCORE _____

LANGUAGE ARTS 607: LIFEPAC TEST

Match the words and phrases (each answer, 2 points).

1. _____ vocabulary   a. insulting remarks

2. _____ recitation bench   b. expected obedience

3. _____ Columbia River   c. province in China

4. _____ Papa   d. Chinese gateboy

5. _____ taunts   e. Presidential

6. _____ sand dunes   f. modifies a noun

7. _____ Shantung   g. person, place, thing

8. _____ Revolutionary War   h. word part

9. _____ Azure Truth   i. words

10. _____ noun   j. burial ground

11. _____ colon   k. school

12. _____ campaign   l. John Day Dam

13. _____ suffix   m. George Washington

14. _____ business letter   n. short, to the point

15. _____ adjective   o. pointing word

     p. used after greeting

Write a word on the blank to correctly complete each sentence (each answer, 3 points).

16. The word *them* is *not* a _____ word.

17. When spelling number words, remember the _____ .

18. A writing in another language is called a _____ .

19. Abraham Lincoln was on his way to the _____ .

20. A business letter has _____ parts.

21. The bandit in "Midnight Callers" said he was going on a long _____ .

Answer true or false (each answer, 2 points).

22. _____ To be successful later, build your vocabulary now.

23. _____ "Broken Bricks" is not a true story.

24. _____ The Warner family named Agate Island.

25. _____ George vowed never to be so irresponsible again.

26. _____ The town of Alderdale still stands on the banks of the Columbia River.

27. _____ Sequential order means to alphabetize events.

28. _____ In the early 1900s China was greatly troubled by warlords and bandits.

29. _____ Missionary Warner was very courteous to the bandit.

30. _____ The soldiers recognized George Washington.

31. _____ A proper noun is capitalized.

32. _____ The possessive forms of nouns and pronouns are often used as adjectives.

33. _____ Kaffir corn sometimes grows as high as fourteen or fifteen feet.

34. _____ Grace Bedell did not like Abraham Lincoln's whiskers.

35. _____ Adjectives always appear before the nouns they describe, limit, or point out.

36. _____ When you write requesting information, you are writing a business letter.

Write a word on the blank to correctly complete each sentence (each answer, 2 points).

colon	inside	meaning
demonstrative	them	trust

37. A suffix can change the _____ of a word.

38. A _____ is used after the greeting in a business letter.

39. The extra part of the business letter is the _____ address.

40. The words, *this*, *that*, *these*, and *those*, are _____ pronouns.

41. The word, _____ , is not a pointing word.

42. Missionary Troxel chose Azure Truth because of his _____ in God.

Complete the following activities (each answer, 5 points).

43. Explain how George Washington showed his greatness.

_____

_____

_____

44. Explain why you think Missionary Troxel chose Azure Truth for the dangerous trip.

_____

_____

_____

ABC **Take your LIFEPAC Spelling Test.**

Complete these spelling activities.

2.64 Write words with the ear pattern from Spelling Words-2. Write them in your very best handwriting.

a. _____   b. _____

c. _____   d. _____

e. _____   f. _____

g. _____   h. _____

i. _____   j. _____

k. _____

2.65 Place the ear words from Spelling Words-2 in the correct column. The ear words have three sound patterns. Say each key word to yourself.

      y ear (yēr)   t ear (tār)   ear n (ern)

a. _____   d. _____   f. _____

b. _____   e. _____   g. _____

c. _____   h. _____

2.66 One ear word could be placed in two columns. Which word is it? _____

2.67 Now find four words in Spelling Words-2 that contain four syllables each.

a. _____

b. _____

c. _____

d. _____

2.68 Find the seven words in Spelling Words-2 from the Bible. Look up Psalm 24 and find each word. Also find an *-ear* word in Psalm 24:4.

a. Psalm 24:2 _____

b. Psalm 24:3 _____

c. Psalm 24:4 _____

d. Psalm 24:4 _____

e. Psalm 24:4 _____

f. Psalm 24:5 _____

g. Psalm 24:6 _____

h. Psalm 24:7 _____

ABC **Ask your teacher to give you a practice spelling test of Spelling Words-2.** Restudy the words you missed.

Handwriting. Make the loops fill the spaces. Keep the downstrokes of the loop letters slanted the same way. Be sure to close the o and do not come back to the line when you join o to the next letter. Watch your beginning and ending strokes. Touch the lines. Write carefully.

Complete these handwriting activities.

2.69 Practice these capital letters.

" The earth is the Lord's and the fulness thereof; the world, and they that dwell therein." Psalm 24 :1

2.70 Write Psalm 24:1 in your very best handwriting. Try for perfection.

_____

_____

_____

_____

_____

_____

2.71 Memorize Psalm 24:1. On a separate sheet of paper, write it from memory.

TEACHER CHECK _____ _____

initials   date

Review the material in this section to prepare for the Self Test. This Self Test will check your understanding of this section and will review the first section. Any items you miss in the following test will show you what areas you need to restudy.

SELF TEST 2

Answer true or false (each answer, 2 points).

2.01 _____ Often God uses little experiences in our childhood to help build character traits.

2.02 _____ The town of Alderdale still stands on the banks of the Columbia River.

2.03 _____ The digraph *ea* has three sounds.

2.04 _____ George couldn't remember what his father wanted him to do.

2.05 _____ When writing, each new word (if not capitalized) should begin with a stroke that starts on the line.

2.06 _____ In the early 1900s China was troubled because of warlords and bandits.

2.07 _____ Successful people have large vocabularies.

2.08 _____ A new missionary in China always learned quickly to obey orders from bandits.

2.09 _____ Baby Wilma started to cry in "Midnight Callers".

2.010 _____ Chinese dollars are paper.

2.011 _____ A noun names a person, place, or thing.

2.012 _____ Missionary Warner offered to make the bandit a cup of tea.

2.013 _____ Missionary Warner was tempted to grab the bandit's gun.

2.014 _____ The bandit was courteous as he left.

2.015 _____ A proper noun begins with a capital letter.

Write a word on the blank to correctly complete each sentence (each answer, 3 points).

2.016 When studying spelling words, break each word into _____ .

2.017 George Segundus was a lazy old _____ .

2.018 The _____ is the order in which things happen in a story.

2.019 Your handwriting gives an _____ of you.

2.020 There were reasons for Missionary Mamma to be _____ .

2.021 The bandit put meaning to his words by bringing out a _____ .

2.022 Missionary Warner led the bandit to the small sack of _____ dollars.

2.023 The robber's whole body was _____ .

2.024 George Washington's soldiers a. _____ and b. _____ him.

2.025 As the bandit stepped out of the door, he too, remembered his _____ .

Write a word from the Word Bank to correctly complete each sentence (each answer, 2 points).

WORD BANK

Alderdale	Indian	strange
China	main	true story
conditions	Revolutionary War	vocabularies
corporal	robber	vowel digraph
fortified	sternly	three

2.026 Words build our _____ .

2.027 "Let George Do It!" is a _____ .

2.028 Vowels working together to make one sound are called a _____ .

2.029 Papa reminded the children they must respect their _____ friends.

2.030 The town of _____ now lies quiet and still beneath the lake formed by John Day Dam.

2.031 "Midnight Callers" takes place in _____ .

2.032 The gateman spoke in a manner that was _____ .

2.033 Rumors said political _____ were at "sevens and eights."

2.034 The *ear* words have _____ sound patterns.

2.035 The purpose of the story is the _____ idea of a story.

2.036 The inexpensive watches missionaries kept on hand were often called

" _____ watches."

2.037 During the _____ George Washington was a general and the commander-in-chief.

2.038 Washington went out to inspect a camp which was to be _____ .

2.039 The _____ shouted at the men again, but he offered them no help.

2.040 Washington turned to the corporal and _____ told him he should have helped his men.

Write the answers in complete sentences (each answer, 5 points).

2.041 Describe how Missionary Warner treated the bandit.

_____

_____

_____

2.042 Explain how George Washington showed his greatness.

_____

_____

_____

_____

80 / 100   SCORE _____   TEACHER _____ _____
                                                 initials   date

ABC   **Take your spelling test of Spelling Words-2.**

3. SECTION THREE

In this section you will continue to practice skills that will help you to understand what you read. You will also study how to recognize words as different kinds of adjectives and suffixes of words. You will also learn to write a business letter.

Section Objectives

Review these objectives. When you have finished this section, you should be able to:

1. Give a definition of a true story.
2. Tell the main details of each reading selection in this LIFEPAC.
3. Arrange the events of each story in this LIFEPAC in the correct order.
4. Identify the clues that indicate the validity of a story or statement.
6. Identify the author's purpose or the main idea of a passage.
8. Spell certain multisyllable words from the Bible.
10. Spell certain number words.
12. Identify the adjectives in a sentence.
13. Identify some suffixes and tell what they mean.
14. Use demonstrative pronouns correctly in written sentences.
15. Write a business letter.

Vocabulary

Study these words to enhance your learning in this section.

campaign (kam pān). A number of connected activities to do something or to get something.

formal (fôr mul). With strict attention to outward forms.

idiotic (id ē ot ik). Very stupid or foolish.

kaffir corn (kaf ur korn). A sorghum grain, which has a stout, short jointed, leafy stalk.

suspend (su spend). To hang down by attaching to something above.

Pronunciation Key: hat, āge, cãre, fär; let, ēqual, tėrm; it, īce; hot, ōpen, ôrder; oil; out; cup, pu̇t, rüle; child; long; thin; /ℱH/ for then; /zh/ for measure; /u/ or /ə/ represents /a/ in about, /e/ in taken, /i/ in pencil, /o/ in lemon, and /u/ in circus.

STORY — "BROKEN BRICKS"

The story you will read takes place in China. The mission needed to cash a check. The bank was located in a distant city. A dangerous journey needed to be made through the robber-infested countryside from the interior city of Nankwan-tao (Nan gwan dou). Who would be chosen to carry these precious rolls of Chinese silver dollars back to the mission station?

Missionary Troxel chose Mr. Chang, whose Chinese name was "Azure Truth." Mr. Chang did not hold a high position in the church. In fact sometimes Mr. Chang did not seem too bright. Why did Mr. Troxel choose "Azure Truth" for this important task? Do you think "Azure Truth" was a good name for this man? Notice the expressions in this story. We do not speak in this manner. These expressions were used to show you more clearly what the translation from the Chinese language would be.

Broken Bricks

by Della Johnson

1 "Azure Truth (Mr. Chang), how are you today? Would your legs carry you many miles to Jade Acres on an errand for me?" asked Missionary Troxel.

2 The face of the Chinese gateboy, Azure Truth Chang, lit up with a smile. "Oh, Pastor, I will go." He was very honored to be asked to perform this task.

3 "But, Chang, this errand could be dangerous. It involves money— the carrying of money. Do you want this responsibility?"

4 "I will bring the money home safely, for I will pray to God. Do not have a '**suspended** heart' (anxiety) while I am gone. All will go well," replied the gateboy. "God will help me."

5 "But, Azure Truth," said Mr. Troxel, "remember it is fall. The **kaffir corn** grows high (sometimes 14-15 feet). You know what that means— bandits are lurking and watching for men carrying money."

6 Azure Truth ran off to put on a clean suit of indigo blue and to put on a fresh towel for his hat. He chose sturdy, cloth-soled shoes, the most comfortable pair for the long trip ahead. When he returned, the missionary was ready with the check to be cashed and a canvas sack in which to carry the money received.

7 Missionary Troxel walked to the city gate with the lad. He prayed with the boy and gave him a loving pat on the shoulder as he passed through the big gate. Would Azure Truth be safe and unharmed? The missionary lifted another prayer as he turned back to the mission compound. Missionary Troxel's heart was deeply touched by Azure Truth's simple faith in God and in him.

8 Azure Truth reached his destination and was ready to start for home. He put the precious rolls of Chinese dollars in the canvas sack and his towel was draped just right over his head.

His belt was tightened to just the right tension about his waist and his shoes were comfortable. Still he hesitated. A strange feeling came over him.

9 "I have been in-heart praying, but now I must kneel-down pray before I start home," he thought.

10 So the errand boy, money bag and all, had a kneel-down prayer time. The place where he prayed was near an old brickyard and kiln. Pieces of old brick were scattered on the ground. As he prayed, something told Azure Truth to pick up a few pieces of old brick that lay nearby and drop them in the bag on top of the precious money. After he was done his heart was at peace, and he started confidently on the long, dusty road home. Azure Truth knew that God was with him.

11 He had not gone far when kaffir corn fields walled him in on both sides of the single-track road. What were those peculiar rustlings he heard? First a head appeared through the green foliage. Then two more heads appeared! Bandits! Bandits! Azure Truth stopped in his tracks. He slid the bag from his shoulder, and smiled his innocent, almost **idiotic** smile at the bandits.

12 "What do you carry in that sack?" roared the bandit leader.

13 "Money," grinned Chang calmly.

14 "Open up, stupid one, let me see."

15 Chang's clumsy hands loosened the sack mouth. The leader of the group peered in. "Bricks! I thought you looked crazy. Now I know you are crazy! We can't waste time or bullets on such a worthless one. Get on your way!"

16 Soon, the bandits had disappeared into the hiding places of the kaffir cornfields. Azure Truth was now alone on a deeply rutted road with a canvas bag full of money and brick fragments. He trudged on his way.

17 In due time Chang reached the mission compound. What a wonderful story he had to tell!

18 "Pastor, I almost despaired when I saw the bandits coming, but God heard our prayers, and they could not hurt me."

19 Missionary Troxel once more placed a loving pat on Chang's shoulder. The missionary said tenderly, "Azure Truth, your trust in God and truthfulness under great temptation is worth more to me than the money you brought safely home. God is a present help to those who put their trust in Him."

"Take a second look; it costs you nothing."

-Chinese Proverb

| Kaffir cornfields walled him in.

Complete the following activities.

3.1   Place an **X** before each statement that reinforces this idea.

Mr. Troxel said, "Azure Truth, your trust in God and truthfulness under great temptation is worth more than money."

a. _____   "I will bring the money home safely for I will pray to God."

b. _____   The kaffir corn grows high.

c. _____   He chose sturdy cloth-soled shoes.

d. _____   "I must kneel-down pray before I start home."

e. _____   He brought the money safely back.

3.2   Place an **X** before each statement that reinforces this statement. The trip was through robber infested countryside.

a. _____   This errand could be dangerous.

b. _____   Mr. Troxel walked to the city gate with the lad.

c. _____   Bandits are lurking and watching for men carrying money.

d. _____   "What do you carry in that sack?" roared the bandit leader.

e. _____   He trudged on his way.

3.3 Number these events in the order in which they happened.

a. _____ Azure Truth ran off to put on a clean suit of indigo blue.

b. _____ Missionary Troxel walked to the city gate with the lad.

c. _____ "Azure Truth, how are your legs today?" asked Missionary Troxel.

d. _____ In due time Chang reached the mission compound.

e. _____ "I will go."

f. _____ The errand boy, money bag and all, had a kneel-down prayer time.

3.4 Place an **X** in front of each word that is a noun. Read again about nouns in Section Two.

a. _____ legs   b. _____ money

c. _____ Jade Acres   d. _____ miles

e. _____ want   f. _____ with

g. _____ Pastor   h. _____ gone

i. _____ God   j. _____ heart

3.5 Read the words again in 3.4 and write the proper nouns.

a. _____

b. _____

c. _____

Answer each question correctly.

3.6 Why was Mr. Troxel concerned about the trip to Jade Acres?

_____

_____

3.7 What is kaffir corn?

_____

_____

3.8 What is a mission compound?

_____

_____

3.9 What made Azure Truth hesitate before returning home?

_____

_____

3.10 What do you think is meant by "in-heart" praying?

_____

_____

3.11 Why did the robbers think Azure Truth was crazy?

_____

_____

3.12 What did Mr. Troxel tell Azure Truth was the most important to him?

_____

_____

TEACHER CHECK _____ _____
                     initials   date

GRAMMAR

The uses of suffixes need frequent review. Adjectives are words used in sentences. They describe or limit words in a variety of ways. Demonstrative pronouns are pronouns that are used like adjectives.

Suffixes. A suffix is a syllable or word part added to the end of the word. Suffixes added to root words make new words. A suffix can change the meaning of a root word. The suffixes _less_ and _ful_ are often used to make new words. Look up the meanings of these two suffixes in your dictionary.

Examples:

fear + less = fearless   fear + ful = fearful

tear + less = tearless   tear + ful = tearful

care + less = careless   care + ful = careful

Here are some other suffixes: -ly, -ous, -ness, -able, -ible.

Complete these activities on suffixes.

3.13 Add suffixes to the following root words to change their meaning.

a. use _____   e. careful _____

b. faith _____   f. strong _____

c. prosper _____   g. respectful _____

d. truth _____   h. joy _____

3.14 Write a sentence using each new word in 3.13 correctly. Have a helper check your sentences.

a. _____

b. _____

c. _____

d. _____

e. _____

f. _____

TEACHER CHECK _____ _____
                                                    initials   date

Adjectives. Adjectives are more difficult to identify than nouns. Adjectives are used in different positions in sentences but they always tell about nouns. Adjectives describe, limit, or point out nouns.

Clue words for an adjective are: is (or are); very ------

You can determine adjectives by their position in relation to nouns.

Example:

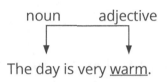

The day is very <u>warm</u>.

The <u>little</u> boy walked away

> Adjectives are words that describe, limit, or point out nouns.

First underline the nouns in each sentence with one line then, underline the adjectives with two lines.

3.15 China was very troubled.

3.16 Azure Truth felt very honored.

3.17 He had very simple faith.

3.18 It is a true story.

3.19 A great God helps us.

Adjectives tell you more about nouns; they can answer the questions what kind? and how many? and which one?

Examples:

Missionary Warner knew that <u>more</u> <u>robbers</u> were outside.

(The adjective *more* tells you how many.)

Azure Truth chose <u>sturdy</u>, <u>cloth-soled</u> <u>shoes</u>.

(The adjectives *sturdy* and *cloth-soled* tell you what kind of shoes.)

Azure Truth picked up pieces of <u>old</u> <u>brick</u>.

(The adjective *old* tells you which brick was picked up.)

Underline the adjectives in these sentences with two lines. Underline the nouns they answer questions about with one line.

3.20 Azure Truth put on a clean suit.

3.21 The missionary gave Azure Truth a loving pat.

3.22 A strange feeling came over him.

3.23 Pieces of old brick were scattered on the ground.

3.24 Three heads appeared.

3.25 He smiled an idiotic smile.

3.26 Chang was alone on the rutted road.

3.27 Chang loosened the sack mouth.

The adjectives *a, an,* and *the* are called *articles.*

A and *an* are called *the indefinite articles. The* is *the definite article.*

In the following sentences, underline each adjective twice and circle each article.

3.28 He ran off to put on a clean shirt.

3.29 He chose the sturdy, cloth-soled shoes.

3.30 The missionary gave him a canvas sack for the money.

3.31 Missionary Troxel walked to the city gate with the lad. Missionary Troxel's heart was deeply touched by Azure Truth's simple faith in God and in him.

3.32 His clumsy hands loosened the sack mouth.

Read this little story about Abraham Lincoln and watch for adjectives.

Most of the pictures we see of tall, lanky Abraham Lincoln show him wearing chin whiskers. Abraham Lincoln did not always wear whiskers.

During Lincoln's Presidential **campaign**, a little girl saw a picture of him. Grace Bedell decided his homely, plain face would look better with whiskers. Grace wrote Abraham Lincoln a letter telling him he would make a good President—but he would look better if he let his whiskers grow.

Lincoln wrote a nice reply to Grace. One day after the election when he was on his way to the inauguration, his train stopped at Westfield, New York.

A large crowd had gathered at the depot. Lincoln asked someone if Grace Bedell was present. Grace shyly pushed her way forward. Lincoln picked her up and kissed her. "I took your advice," he said. "Now, see what I look like." Lincoln held her up for the crowd to see. The delighted crowd cheered loudly and waved their hats.

Look in the story for these adjectives.

3.33 Find two adjectives describing Abraham Lincoln.

a. _____ b. _____

3.34 What kind of a campaign was mentioned? _____

3.35 Find two adjectives that described Abraham Lincoln's face.

a. _____ b. _____

3.36 Grace Bedell thought Lincoln would make what kind of President? _____

3.37 What size girl was Grace? _____

3.38 Describe the crowd at the depot when Lincoln held up Grace. _____

Words that show possession show who something belongs to. Possessive nouns and possessive pronouns are often used to do the work of adjectives. Some examples of possessive pronouns were given in Section Two. Study these examples of a possessive noun and of a possessive pronoun.

Examples: The night watchman's voice did not sound familiar.
His name was Azure Truth.

Underline the possessive nouns or pronouns used as adjectives.

3.39 Azure Truth's suit was indigo blue.

3.40 Missionary Troxel's heart was deeply touched.

3.41 His towel was draped just right over his head.

3.42 His belt was tightened to just the right tension about his waist.

3.43 Chang's clumsy hands loosened the sack mouth.

3.44 God honored Azure Truth's faith.

Many adjectives change in form to express comparison. Two people may be tall, but one person is *taller* than the other. *Taller* is the *comparative form*. When you wish to compare more than two things, use the *superlative form*.

Examples: Jack is tall.

Jim is taller than Jack.   comparing two

Jim is the tallest boy in the class.   comparing more than two

 Write the correct form of the adjective.

Adjective	Comparative (*er*)	Superlative (*est*)
3.45 short	_____	_____
3.46 cheap	_____	_____
3.47 hard	_____	_____
3.48 fat	_____	_____
3.49 sweet	_____	_____
3.50 quiet	_____	_____

Write a sentence using the comparative and a sentence using the superlative form of each of the words given.

3.51 short   a. comparative   _____

               b. superlative   _____

3.52 cheap   a. comparative   _____

               b. superlative   _____

3.53 hard   a. comparative   _____

               b. superlative   _____

3.54 fat   a. comparative   _____

               b. superlative   _____

3.55 sweet   a. comparative   _____

               b. superlative   _____

3.56 quiet   a. comparative   _____

               b. superlative   _____

TEACHER CHECK _____ _____

                                     initials   date

Demonstrative pronouns. The four pronouns that identify which of two or more things is meant are called *demonstrative pronouns*. *This, that, these,* and *those* are the demonstrative pronouns. They are sometimes called *pointing words*. *This* and *that* are singular; *these* and *those* are plural.

REMEMBER: You do not use two words to point out the same thing at one time.

> To use *here* with *this* or *these* is incorrect.
>
> To use *there* with *that* or *those* is incorrect.

Right:	This wood is hard.
Wrong:	This here wood is solid.

> *Them* is not a pointing word.

Sometimes people use the word *them* as a pointing word when they should use *these* or *those*. *Them* is not a pointing word.

Right:	I made these shelves.
Right:	I made those shelves.
Wrong:	I made them shelves.

> Do not use *these* and *those* with *kind*.

Often people say *these kind* or *those kind* when they should say *this kind* or *that kind*. The word *kind* is singular.

The words *this* and *that* are used to tell or ask about only one.

Kinds is used to tell or ask about more than one. Use *these* or *those* with *kinds*.

Right:	I like this (or that) kind of cake.
Wrong:	I like these (or those) kinds of cake.
Right:	The bakery makes all these (or those) kinds of cakes.

✎ **Write the correct word in each blank. Cross out the words _here_ or _there_ in any sentence where they are used incorrectly.**

3.57 Do you like _____ here games?
                        (this, these)

3.58 No, I don't like _____ games.
                        (those, them)

3.59 (That, Those, Them) _____ kind is too easy to play.

3.60 Have you seen _____ there new ones that Sam has?
                        (those, them)

3.61 Are they harder to play than _____ here?
                                    (this, these)

3.62 Ben bought _____ there kind we saw at the store.
                    (that, those, them)

3.63 They are just like _____ that I want.
                            (those, them)

BUSINESS LETTERS

When you write a person or a company requesting information or ordering something, you are writing a business letter.

Many times when you write a business letter, you do not know the person at all. A letter you write to someone you do not know well would be written in a more **formal** way than a friendly letter. Business letters must be written in a certain form.

The business letter has six parts, one more part than the friendly letter. A business letter should be short and to the point. If you do not know the name of the person to whom you are writing, use the greeting "Gentlemen." The part included in the business letter that is not included in the friendly letter is the "inside address." The inside address includes the name and address of the person or company to whom you are writing. The inside address is written before the greeting. This name and address also appears on the envelope.

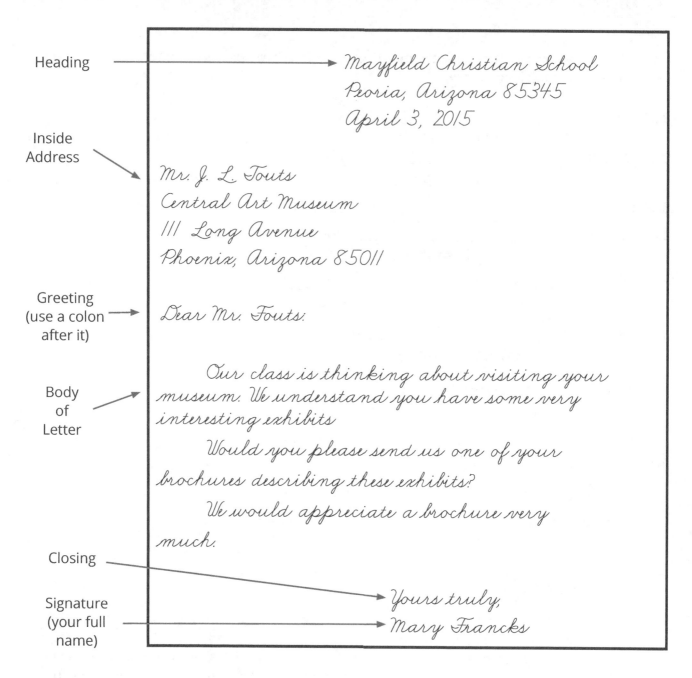

Heading — *Mayfield Christian School*
Peoria, Arizona 85345
April 3, 2015

Inside Address — *Mr. J. L. Fouts*
Central Art Museum
111 Long Avenue
Phoenix, Arizona 85011

Greeting (use a colon after it) — *Dear Mr. Fouts:*

Body of Letter — *Our class is thinking about visiting your museum. We understand you have some very interesting exhibits*
Would you please send us one of your brochures describing these exhibits?
We would appreciate a brochure very much.

Closing — *Yours truly,*

Signature (your full name) — *Mary Francks*

Answer the following questions.

3.64 What are the six parts of a business letter?

a. _____   b. _____

c. _____   d. _____

e. _____   f. _____

3.65 A business letter has one more part than a friendly letter. What is it? _____

3.66 What punctuation should you use after the greeting? _____

3.67 Why is the second part of the letter called the inside address?

_____

_____

Choose one of the following projects and write a business letter.

3.68 a. Write a letter to a make-believe company requesting more information about a subject.
      b. Look in magazines and newspapers for trips that are advertised or for booklets about interesting places to visit. Write a letter requesting information.

_____

_____

_____

_____

_____

_____

_____

_____

_____

_____

_____

_____

_____

_____

_____

_____

_____

_____

_____

TEACHER CHECK _____ _____
                                          initials   date

SPELLING AND HANDWRITING

This spelling study will help you to learn more of the words that are used in the Bible. In addition, you will learn which number words to hyphenate. In handwriting you will practice joining letters into words.

Spelling. Psalm 46 provides eight words for Spelling Words-3. Three of the words in the list are cardinal numbers and three words are ordinal numbers.

Review the rules given in Section One for studying spelling words.

SPELLING WORDS-3

cease	destruction	forty-six	refuge
chariot	eightieth	heathen	sixty-eight
confidently	exalted	midst	tabernacle
dangerous	fiftieth	missionary	translation
desolations	first	position	twenty-two

Look for six number words in Spelling Words-3. Notice which of these number words have hyphens. It is important to remember the rule. Hyphenate numbers when combining tens and ones.

> When writing the numbers twenty-one to ninety-nine, use hyphens.

The hyphen is important! One time in a spelling contest, a girl missed the championship by leaving out the hyphen in a number word.

Complete these spelling activities.

3.69 Write each number word from Spelling Words-3 in a sentence.

a. _____

b. _____

c. _____

d. _____

e. _____

f. _____

3.70 Eight of the words from Spelling Words-3 come from Psalm 46.

Read Psalm 46 and find each word.

a. Psalm 46:1 _____

b. Psalm 46:4 _____

c. Psalm 46:5 _____

d. Psalm 46:6 _____

e. Psalm 46:8 _____

f. Psalm 46:9 _____

g. Psalm 46:9 _____

h. Psalm 46:10 _____

3.71 In the introductory paragraphs of the story, "Broken Bricks," find a word that means *a writing in another language.* _____

3.72 In the first paragraph of the story, "Broken Bricks," find a word that tells what Mr. Troxel was.

_____

3.73 In the third paragraph of "Broken Bricks," find a word that means *might bring harm.*

_____

3.74 In the second introductory paragraph of the story, "Broken Bricks," find a word that means *where a person is placed in relation to others.* _____

3.75 In the tenth paragraph find a word that means *in a very self confident manner.*

_____

3.76 In the eleventh paragraph of the story, "Broken Bricks," find a word that tells you *that something happened before any others.* _____

Complete the puzzle.

3.77 The clues for this puzzle are definitions for fourteen of the words in Spelling Words-3.

Find these words!

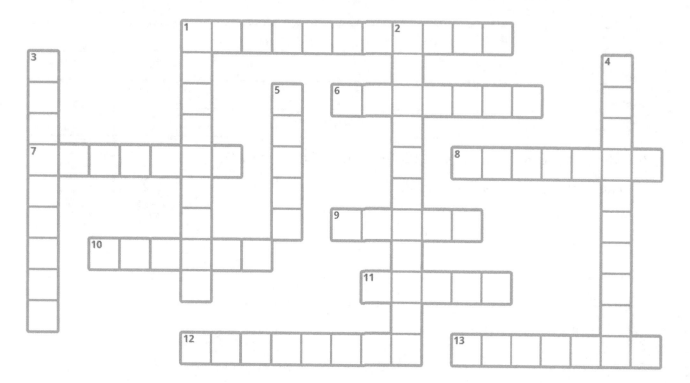

Across

1. Damage so as to make useless
6. A two-wheeled vehicle
7. A person who does not worship God
8. Made high in rank, honor, or power
9. To stop
10. A shelter
11. In the middle
12. Placement
13. Promoted

Down

1. Full of danger
2. The result of changing into another language
3. An ordinal number for *eighty*
4. A place of worship
5. Foremost

ABC **Ask your teacher to give you a practice spelling test of Spelling Words-3.** Restudy the words you missed.

Handwriting. Review what you studied in the first two sections about handwriting. Writing another Bible verse will give you practice in putting letters together.

Complete these handwriting activities.

3.78 Practice the following letters.

_G_

_p_

_h_

Mr. Troxel used words from Psalm 46:1. Study the way this verse is written.

"God is our refuge and strength, a very present help in trouble." Psalm 46:1

3.79 Write Psalm 46:1. Remember to write the quotation marks, comma, and period.

Before taking the last Self Test, you may want to do one or more of these self checks.

1. _____ Read the objectives. See if you can do them.
2. _____ Restudy the material related to any objectives that you cannot do.
3. _____ Use the **SQ3R** study procedure to review the material.
   a. **S**can the sections.
   b. **Q**uestion yourself.
   c. **R**ead to answer your questions.
   d. **R**ecite the answers to yourself.
   e. **R**eview areas you did not understand.
4. _____ Review all vocabulary, activities, and Self Tests, writing a correct answer for every wrong answer

SELF TEST 3

Answer true or false (each answer, 2 points).

3.01 _____ George Warner became a missionary in China.

3.02 _____ George vowed never to take a boat ride on the Columbia again.

3.03 _____ The digraph *ea* has three sounds.

3.04 _____ In the early 1900s China was greatly troubled because of war lords and bandits.

3.05 _____ The gateman's voice sounded strange.

3.06 _____ The bandit wanted money.

3.07 _____ Mr. Warner grabbed the bandit's gun.

3.08 _____ The bandit killed Fien Feng.

3.09 _____ Mr. Warner was courteous to the bandits.

3.010 _____ Mr. Chang held a high position in the church.

3.011 _____ Mr. Troxel was afraid the bank would not cash the check.

3.012 _____ Azure Truth carried the money in a canvas sack.

3.013 _____ Mr. Troxel walked to the city gate with the lad.

3.014 _____ Azure Truth prayed near an old brick yard.

3.015 _____ The bandits stopped Chang because they thought he had bricks in the bag.

Write a word on the blank to correctly complete each sentence (each answer, 3 points).

3.016 A Chinese proverb says, "Take a second _____ ; it costs you nothing."

3.017 When writing the numbers twenty-one to ninety-nine, use a _____ .

3.018 The order in which one event follows another is called the _____ .

3.019 During Lincoln's Presidential _____ , a little girl saw a picture of Abraham Lincoln.

3.020 Grace Bedell decided Abraham Lincoln's _____ face would look better with whiskers.

3.021 On Lincoln's way to the _____ , his train stopped at Westfield, New York.

3.022 Lincoln picked up Grace Bedell and _____ her.

3.023 When you write to a person or a company requesting information or ordering something, you are writing a _____ letter.

3.024 A business letter has _____ parts.

3.025 A friendly letter has _____ parts.

Write a word from the Word Bank to correctly complete each sentence (each answer, 2 points).

WORD BANK
---

adjectives	kind	purposefully
comparative	limit	story
definite	pointing	suffixes
formal	political	superlative
indefinite	pronoun	vocabularies

3.026 We should read _____ and wisely.

3.027 Words build our _____ .

3.028 A business letter is more _____ than a friendly letter.

3.029 The word *the* is the _____ article.

3.030 "Let George Do It!" is a true _____ .

3.031 The words *a* and *an* are called _____ articles.

3.032 Rumors said that in China _____ conditions were at "sevens and eights."

3.033 When comparing more than two things, use the _____ form of an adjective.

3.034 The *er* ending is the _____ form of an adjective.

3.035 Adjectives are words that describe, _____ , or point out nouns.

3.036 Possessive forms of nouns and pronouns are often used as _____ .

3.037 New words are made by adding _____ .

3.038 *This, that, these,* and *those* are demonstrative _____ .

3.039 Demonstrative pronouns are sometimes called _____ words.

3.040 Do not use *these* and *those* with _____ .

Complete the following activities (each answer, 5 points).

3.041 Explain why you think Missionary Troxel chose Azure Truth for the dangerous trip.

_____

_____

3.042 List the six parts of a business letter.

a. _____   b. _____

c. _____   d. _____

e. _____   f. _____

80 / 100   SCORE _____   TEACHER _____ _____
                                              initials   date

ABC

Take your spelling test of Spelling Words-3.

Before taking the LIFEPAC Test, you may want to do one or more of these self checks.

1. _____ Read the objectives. See if you can do them.
2. _____ Restudy the material related to any objectives that you cannot do.
3. _____ Use the **SQ3R** study procedure to review the material.
4. _____ Review activities, Self Tests, and LIFEPAC vocabulary words.
5. _____ Restudy areas of weakness indicated by the last Self Test.
6. _____ Review all Spelling Words in this LIFEPAC.

LANGUAGE ARTS 608
Analyzing the News

LIFEPAC Test is located in the center of the booklet. Please remove before starting the unit.

Author:
Lila Vance Langford, M.A.

Editor-in-Chief:
Richard W. Wheeler, M.A.Ed.

Editor:
Helen Robertson Prewitt, M.A.Ed.

Consulting Editor:
Rudolph Moore, Ph.D.

Revision Editor:
Alan Christopherson, M.S.

MEDIA CREDITS:

Page 7: © Jana Krcmarova, iStock, Thinkstock; **17:** © Michael Blann, Digital Vision, Thinkstock; **24:** © Tribalium, iStock, Thinkstock; **28:** © Oleg Saenko, Hemera; **40:** © triloks, iStock, Thinkstock.

Alpha Omega
PUBLICATIONS

804 N. 2nd Ave. E.
Rock Rapids, IA 51246-1759

Analyzing the News

Introduction

In this LIFEPAC® you will learn about newspapers both in print and online. You will study the history of newspapers, the importance of newspapers, and the power of propaganda. You will identify main ideas and judge propaganda used in communications media. You will also learn some newspaper terms, learn to analyze a news story, and write a news story of your own.

You will study about auxiliary verbs, contractions of verbs, tenses of verbs, and verb phrases. You will also study adverbs and the comparative forms of adjectives.

As you study this LIFEPAC, you will continue to build your spelling and handwriting skills.

Objectives

Read the following objectives. The objectives tell you what you should be able to do when you have successfully completed this LIFEPAC. Each section will list according to the numbers below what objectives will be met in that section. When you have finished the following LIFEPAC, you should be able to:

1. Explain how to select the main idea of an article, a story, or a report.

2. Identify and explain the difference between fact and opinion.

3. Recognize and use verbs.

4. Explain the function of a verb.

5. Form some verb tenses.

6. Describe the power and the pattern of propaganda.

7. Explain the meaning of the word *internalize*.

8. Identify and use auxiliary verbs.

9. Identify and use verb phrases.

10. Form verb contractions.

11. List the parts of a news story.

12. Explain how analyze a news story.

13. Identify and use adverbs.

14. Identify and use adverb phrases.

15. Define and spell new words.

16. Practice handwriting skills.

Survey the LIFEPAC. Ask yourself some questions about this study and write your questions here.

1. SECTION ONE

Reading a brief history of newspapers may sharpen your awareness of the importance of news media. In this LIFEPAC you will study the history of newspapers. You will select the main idea of an article and explain the difference between fact and **opinion**. **Propaganda** is another topic you will study. You will use your local newspaper to help you in this LIFEPAC. You will analyze a news story and write one of your own.

Grammar is also included in this LIFEPAC. You will review the uses of verbs. You will learn more about tense, auxiliary verbs, and verb phrases. You will also study about adverbs and adverb phrases.

You will improve your spelling and handwriting skills. You will learn to spell newspaper terms, language arts terms, and comparisons of adjectives. In handwriting you will practice writing words with difficult joinings of *w* and *v*.

Section Objectives

Review these objectives. When you have completed this section, you should be able to:

1. Explain how to select the main idea of an article, a story, or a report.
2. Identify and explain the difference between fact and opinion.
3. Recognize and use verbs.
4. Explain the function of a verb.
5. Form some verb tenses.
15. Define and spell new words.
16. Practice handwriting skills.

Vocabulary

Study these words to enhance your learning success in this section.

adage (ad' ij). A well-known proverb.

ancestor (an' ses tur). Person from whom one is descended.

gregarious (gru gãr' ē us). Fond of being with others.

media (mē' dē u). Plural of medium.

medium (mē' dē um). Substance or agent through which anything acts; a means of communicating thoughts, ideas or opinions.

propaganda (prop u gan' du). A method used deliberately to influence people to believe certain ideas or to follow certain courses of action.

Note: *All vocabulary words in this LIFEPAC appear in* **boldface** *print the first time they are used. If you are unsure of the meaning when you are reading, study the definitions given.*

Pronunciation Key: hat, āge, cãre, fär; let, ēqual, tėrm; it, īce; hot, ōpen, ôrder; oil; out; cup, pu̇t, rüle; child; long; thin; /ŦH/ for then; /zh/ for measure; /u/ or /ə/ represents /a/ in about, /e/ in taken, /i/ in pencil, /o/ in lemon, and /u/ in circus.

THE NEWSPAPER

The article you will read is a brief history of newspapers. Every article has a *main idea*. The main idea tells *the most important thing the writer wants you to know from the article*. As you read this short history, decide on the main idea.

NEWSPAPERS: NOTEWORTHY NECESSITIES

An old **adage** says, "Necessity is the mother of invention." Because people are **gregarious**, they want to know what others are doing and thinking. They need a means for telling the news. Tribes in Africa relayed news across large areas of the country by beating drums. Ancient Egyptians, Assyrians, Babylonians, and Mayas carved important events on monuments. Alexander the Great and Caesar used runners to send news of their triumphs to the citizens of Greece and Rome.

A comparatively modern **medium** of communication is the newspaper. A newspaper is a publication devoted to telling recent happenings and information of general interest.

Perhaps the first recognizable **ancestor** of the newspaper was a handwritten epistle, the newsletter. Appearing in Rome as early as 449 B.C., it recorded the work of the government. Deposited in the Temple of Ceres, copies were made available particularly to officials and wealthy Romans. Added later were sporting events, political news, and social events. These newsletters were inscribed by educated enslaved people. Had it not been for the abundance of slave labor, the printing press might have been invented earlier. Later, in 60 B.C., Julius Caesar ordered the daily news to be recorded and posted in the Forum.

The earliest record of a *printed* newspaper is the *Ti Chan (The Peking Gazette)* in China. It may have been established as early as A.D. 500 and was printed until 1935. This newspaper was produced from carved wood blocks rather than type. Gutenberg's invention of printing from movable type in A.D. 1440 encouraged the development of newspapers in Europe in the fifteenth century. These papers hardly resembled present-day publications because they usually consisted of only one to four pages often printed on only one side.

The beginning of newspaper printing in England—and in the English language—occurred on December 20, 1620, with George Veseler's untitled news sheet. What a **scoop** he would have enjoyed had he known that fellow Englishmen—Pilgrims—had that same day landed in the New World to establish a colony that later became part of the United States of America!

In the American colonies, the first newspaper was a four-page sheet printed in Boston on September 25, 1690, by Richard Pierce. In this one and only **edition**, a leading story told that "the christianized Indians in some parts of Plymouth have newly appointed a day of Thanksgiving to God for his Mercy in supplying their extreme and pinching Necessities under their late want of Corn, & for His giving them a very Comfortable Harvest." The publisher, however, had not obtained a license to publish. Accordingly, the governor **suppressed** his paper. Fourteen years would pass before any other colonist would attempt publication of a newspaper.

In eighteenth-century America, several people published newspapers. One of these papers was *The Pennsylvania Gazette* by Benjamin Franklin. By the outbreak of the American Revolutionary War in 1775, thirty-five papers were being published in the colonies.

When the founders of the new nation, the United States of America, wrote the Constitution, they eventually included the first ten amendments (also called the Bill of Rights).

This addition is a clear definition of the rights and privileges of American citizens. The First Amendment reads, "Congress shall make no law respecting an establishment of religion, or prohibiting the free exercise thereof; or abridging the freedom of speech, or of the press; or the right of the people peaceably to assemble, and to petition the Government for a redress of grievances." Since December 15, 1791, freedom of the press has become an American tradition, not enjoyed by many peoples over the world who are still under news **censorship**.

Answer true or false.

1.1 _____ Gregarious people are not very friendly.

1.2 _____ Ancient Europeans relayed news by beating drums.

1.3 _____ The newspaper is a comparatively modern medium of communication.

1.4 _____ The Roman newsletter, that recorded the work of the Senate as early as 449 B.C., was an ancestor of the newspaper.

1.5 _____ The *Ti Chan* was the first recorded newspaper printed from type.

WORD BANK
---

scoop	the first ten amendments	gazette
censorship	*Pennsylvania Gazette*	edition

Using the Word Bank fill in the blanks.

1.6 All the copies of a newspaper printed alike and issued at nearly the same time are from the same _____ .

1.7 One newspaper gets a _____ when it publishes a news story before another paper does.

1.8 A country or group of people who do not have the freedom to read honest news reports are under _____ .

Finding the main idea. To find the main idea of an article or story you should look for the topic sentence in each paragraph. Notice any important ideas in that paragraph as you quickly look over it and move on to the next paragraph. Put together the ideas from all the paragraphs, and you will have the main idea of the whole article or story.

 Complete this activity.

1.9 Skim the article, "Newspapers: Noteworthy Necessities," to determine the main idea. Put an **X** in front of the sentence that best states the main idea.

a. _____ Newspapers add quality to life.

b. _____ Newspapers emerged to meet a need in people's lives.

c. _____ Publishing a newspaper is hard work.

d. _____ Freedom of the press is guaranteed by the Bill of Rights.

Determining fact or opinion. News stories are generally based on fact—the actual events, situations, persons, or details involved. Whenever a person makes comments about facts, they are expressing an opinion—their feelings or attitudes about something.

 Define the following words.

1.10 Write the definitions of *fact* and *opinion*.

a. fact _____

_____

b. opinion _____

_____

Complete the following activities.

1.11 In the blank before each statement place an *F* if the sentence is *fact*; put an *O* if it is *opinion*.

    a. _____ Tribes in Africa relay news over large areas by beating drums.

    b. _____ Because people are gregarious, they want to know what others are doing and thinking.

    c. _____ The newsletters were inscribed by educated enslaved people.

    d. _____ Freedom of the press has become an American tradition.

    e. _____ Had it not been for the abundance of slave labor, the printing press might have been invented earlier.

1.12 Look at a copy of your local newspaper either in print or online and answer these questions.

    a. What is the name of the paper?

    _____

    b. Who is the editor?

    _____

    c. Who is the publisher?

    _____

    d. How often is it published?

    _____

    e. Which section of the paper do you enjoy most? _____

1.13 Write a paper.

    a. Use an encyclopedia or online resource to look up information about newspapers or journalism today.

    b. On a separate sheet of paper write several paragraphs about your findings.

TEACHER CHECK _____ _____
                                initials   date

VERBS

Verbs have three important jobs: they may express action, they may show state of being, or they may link a noun to another word in the sentence.

Action verbs express some movement or action of the subject. Many words are action verbs: *run, walk, play, think,* and *write.* Any word telling what you do is an action verb.

> I often *bowl* and *swim.*
>
> He *collects* model airplanes.

Being verbs are used to show what a person or thing *is.* Only eight words are in this group: *am, are, be, being, been, is, was, were.*

> I *am* a student.
>
> They *are* absent today.
>
> She *was* ill.

Linking verbs are verbs that join or link the subject and another word in the sentence. Some words in this group are *become, seem, remain, look, feel, taste, smell, appear, sound.*

 Complete the following activities.

1.14 Circle the action verbs in these sentences and write these verbs on the lines.

a. _____ Teletype machines bring the news from around the world to newspapers.

b. _____ News services supply the news.

c. _____ Editors determine the banner headline for the front page.

d. _____ They check the stories for that page.

e. _____ They decide the position of each story.

1.15 Circle the being verbs in these sentences and write these verbs on the lines.

a. _____ News is the paper's life blood.

b. _____ Reporters and photographers are on the staff.

c. _____ Newsprint is the most costly material in the paper.

d. _____ China was the inventor of paper.

e. _____ Publishers were men of conviction.

Complete this activity.

1.16 Circle the linking verbs in these sentences and write these verbs on the lines.

a. _____ Newspapers became a tradition early in our nation.

b. _____ Special features often appear interesting.

c. _____ The comic pages seem popular for many readers.

d. _____ Sports remain a big section.

e. _____ Good editors feel a distinct responsibility for truthful reporting.

Verbs are very important parts of sentences. A sentence must have both a subject and a verb (or predicate).

To find the *subject* of a sentence, ask:

"Who or what is doing or being something in this sentence?"

To find the *predicate* of a sentence, ask:

"Which word (or words) is telling what the subject is doing or being?"

> The *function* (or job) of a verb or verb phrase is to be the *predicate* of a sentence.

Read the following example sentences.

1. Jerry/ is my brother. (*Jerry* is the subject and *is my brother* is the complete predicate.)

2. Lori/ sings beautifully. (*Lori* is the subject and *sings beautifully* is the complete predicate.)

3. Ken and Jon/ play baseball every Saturday. (*Ken and Jon* is the complete subject and *play baseball every Saturday* is the complete predicate.)

Complete the following activity.

1.17 Put a / between the complete subject and the complete predicate in these sentences. Circle the verbs. Above each verb write *v* for action verb, *be* for being verbs, and *LV* for linking verb.

a. Caesar Augustus issued a decree.

b. It was a census.

c. Mary and Joseph registered in Bethlehem.

d. Their home was in Nazareth.

e. Mary bore Jesus.

f. She laid him in a manger.

g. Angels appeared to shepherds in the field.

h. They sang a song of joy.

i. The shepherds worshiped Jesus.

j. This story is the Good News.

Verbs show the time something happens. The time shown by verbs is called tense. Two often used tenses are present tense and past tense. Present tense verbs describe things in the present.

Present tense: I *see* you.
                  Can *you* go?
                  I *swim* every day.

When you form the present tense, you will notice that you must use the personal pronouns with the verb. These personal pronouns are the ones you will be using.

	Singular	*Plural*
First person (speaker)	I	we
Second person (person spoken to)	you	you
Third person (person, thing spoken about)	he, she, it	they

Notice the way these personal pronouns are used with verbs.

	Singular	*Plural*
First person:	I go	we go
Second person:	you go	you go
Third person:	he, it, she goes	they go

All of the forms of the verb *to go* are alike in the present tense, except for the third person singular.

In the following chart you will notice that the "s" form of the present tense is used *only* with the third person singular (he, she, it). Remember, in a word ending with a consonant and *y*, you must change the *y* to *i* and add -*es* (try → tries, fry → fries). Read over the steps for forming the third person singular form of the verb in the present tense.

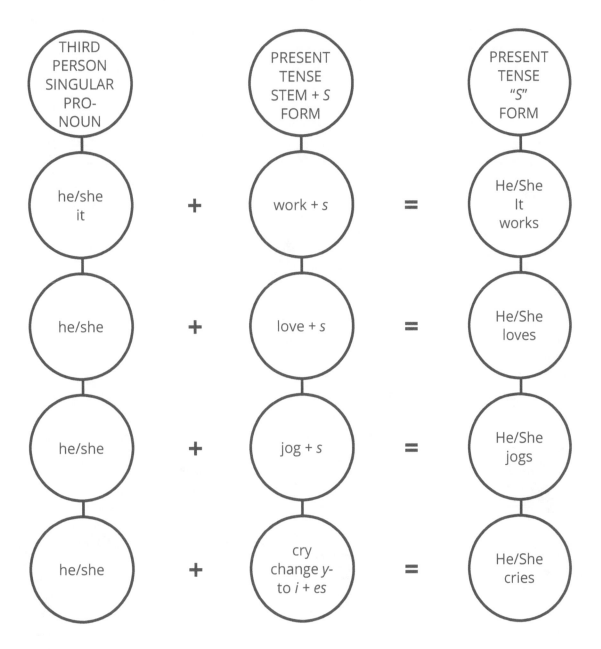

Write the third person form of the verb.

1.18 I work, you work, he _____ .

1.19 I play, you play, he _____ .

1.20 I run, you run, she _____ .

1.21 I jump, you jump, she _____ .

1.22 I study, you study, he _____ .

1.23 I mix, you mix, it _____ .

Present tense verbs are used as the root or base word for making other tenses.

Past tense verbs describe things in the past—two minutes ago, yesterday, last week, or one hundred years ago.

Past tense: He *played* the piano last night.
              She *studied* for her test.
              It *rained* all night.

The past tense for regular verbs is formed by adding *-ed* to the present (root or base) form.

Study the following chart on the next page. Pay attention to any spelling changes.

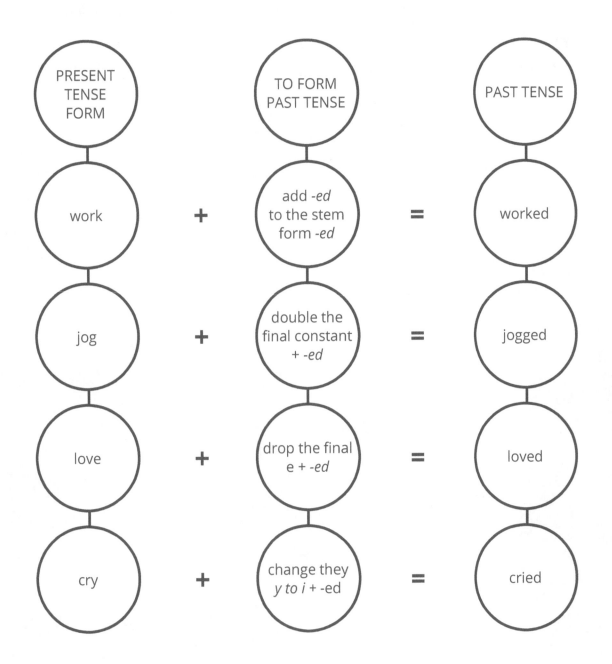

PRESENT TENSE FORM		TO FORM PAST TENSE		PAST TENSE
work	+	add *-ed* to the stem form *-ed*	=	worked
jog	+	double the final constant + *-ed*	=	jogged
love	+	drop the final e + *-ed*	=	loved
cry	+	change they *y to i* + -ed	=	cried

Write the past tense for the following verbs.

1.24 I study, I _____ .

1.25 He studies, he _____ .

1.26 You pray, you _____ .

1.27 We mix, we _____ .

1.28 She arrives, she _____ .

1.29 It snows, it _____ .

Circle the verb in each of the following sentences and write the tense on the line.

1.30 They walked to Bethlehem. _____

1.31 Mary treasured these things in her heart. _____

1.32 We read these words now. _____

1.33 Later Wise Men carried gifts to Jesus. _____

1.34 They returned to Nazareth. _____

SPELLING AND HANDWRITING

In this section you will practice writing words that contain *w* and *v*. The spelling list contains adjectives, language arts terms, and newspaper terms.

Spelling. Adjectives can be used to compare people or things.

A boy may be *small*.
His friend may be *smaller* than he.
His sister may be the *smallest* of all the group.

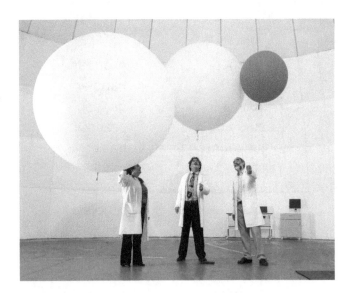

Each step or degree of comparison has a special name.
The first adjective, the root or base form of the word, is called the *positive* degree.

   Positive degree: small, large, cold, hot, wet, happy

To compare two persons or things use the *comparative* degree.
The comparative degree is formed by adding *-er* to the root word (positive degree).
Remember your spelling rules: change the *y* to *i* before adding *-er* or *-est*.

positive degree (root word)	+	*-er*	=	comparative degree
small	+	*-er*	=	smaller
cold	+	*-er*	=	colder
happy	+	*-er*	=	happier

   He is *smaller* than Joe.
   January is *colder* than October.

To compare more than two objects or things use the *superlative* degree of the adjective.
The superlative degree is formed by adding *-est* to the root word (positive degree).

positive degree (root word)	+	*-est*	=	superlative degree
small	+	*-est*	=	smallest
cold	+	*-est*	=	coldest
happy	+	*-est*	=	happiest

   Lori is the *smallest* girl in the class.
   Alaska may be the *coldest* state.
   When Corry made 100 on his spelling test, he was the *happiest* boy in the room.

Learn the meanings and spellings of the words in Spelling Words-1.

SPELLING WORDS-1

newspaper	pronoun	paragraph	necessity
adjective	happier	ancestor	verb
friendliest	banner	adverb	nobler
censorship	preposition	cleverer	edition
conjunction	busier	interview	interjection
craziest	media	sentence	quieter
opinion	subject	gentlest	noun
predicate	simplest		

Complete the following activities.

1.35 In your best handwriting alphabetize your spelling list.

a. _____   b. _____

c. _____   d. _____

e. _____   f. _____

g. _____   h. _____

i. _____   j. _____

k. _____   l. _____

m. _____   n. _____

o. _____   p. _____

q. _____   r. _____

s. _____   t. _____

u. _____   v. _____

w. _____   x. _____

y. _____   z. _____

aa. _____   bb. _____

cc. _____   dd. _____

1.36 List the words that refer to newspapers.

a. _____   b. _____

c. _____   d. _____

e. _____   f. _____

g. _____

1.37 Write the words that are language arts terms.

a. _____   b. _____

c. _____   d. _____

e. _____   f. _____

g. _____   h. _____

i. _____   j. _____

k. _____   l. _____

1.38 Complete the following chart.

	Positive	Comparative	Superlative
a.	happy	_____	_____
b.	_____	nobler	_____
c.	_____	_____	friendliest
d.	busy	_____	_____
e.	_____	crazier	_____
f.	_____	_____	quietest
g.	clever	_____	_____
h.	_____	gentler	_____
i.	simple	_____	_____

ABC   **Ask your teacher to give you a practice spelling test of Spelling Words-1.** Restudy the words you missed.

Handwriting. Be sure to write the entire *w* or *v* before forming the next letter in these words. Be careful in joining these letters with the rest of the word.

Complete the following handwriting activity.

1.39 Write one line of each word. Watch your *w's* and *v's*.

newspaper

invention

devoted

available

known

world

eventually

envied

ways

written

TEACHER CHECK _____ _____

initials   date

↺ **Review the material in this section in preparation for the Self Test.** The Self Test will check your mastery of this particular section. The items missed on this Self Test will indicate specific areas where restudy is needed for mastery.

SELF TEST 1

Complete these statements (each answer, 3 points).

1.01 A person who likes to be with others is said to be _____ .

1.02 A comparatively modern _____ of communication is the newspaper.

1.03 A handwritten epistle, the a. _____ , was the first recognizable

b. _____ of the newspaper.

1.04 Early newsletters were inscribed by educated _____ .

1.05 Earliest printed newspapers appeared in _____ .

1.06 Printing with movable type, invented by _____ , brought newspapers to Europe.

1.07 An early newspaperman in the United States was _____ .

1.08 The first ten amendments of the Constitution, known as the a. _____ ,

guarantee b. _____ .

Complete this activity (this answer, 4 points).

1.09 Write the main idea of this paragraph.

Since December 15, 1791, freedom of the press has become an American tradition, envied by many people over the world who are still under repressive censorship.

_____

_____

Write *F* in the blank if the statement is fact; *O* if it is opinion (each answer, 2 points).

1.010 _____ Newspapers improve life.

1.011 _____ Educated enslaved people inscribed early newsletters.

1.012 _____ China printed newspapers with carved blocks rather than type.

1.013 _____ Freedom of the press is guaranteed by the Bill of Rights in the United States.

Put a slash mark / between the subject and predicate, and label the verb this way:
v over action verbs, *be* above being verbs, and *LV* over linking verbs (each part, 2 points).

1.014 Herod arrested Peter.

1.015 He placed him in prison.

1.016 People in the church prayed.

1.017 An angel awakened Peter.

1.018 Peter seemed in a dream.

1.019 They walked from the prison.

1.020 Peter was grateful for the angel.

1.021 He knocked on John Mark's door.

1.022 Rhoda recognized his voice.

1.023 The praying people challenged her.

1.024 They finally opened the door for him.

1.025 He reported God's miracle.

Write the past tense of the verb in parentheses (each answer, 2 points).

1.026 (preach)   Elijah _____ to his people.

1.027 (blame)   The Pharaoh _____ Moses.

1.028 (receive)   Moses _____ the law.

1.029 (like)   Joshua and Caleb _____ the Promised Land.

1.030 (remain)   Daniel _____ true to God.

80 / 100   **SCORE** _____   **TEACHER** _____ _____
initials   date

ABC   **Take your spelling test of Spelling Words-1.**

2. SECTION TWO

In this section you will read an article about propaganda that may help you realize the power of the written word. You will identify the main idea of the article and will learn to identify and to judge propaganda used in various media.

In this section you will also learn more about verbs. You will study auxiliary verbs and contractions of verbs with *not*.

You will also improve your spelling and handwriting skills. You will learn to spell science terms and more newspaper terms. In handwriting you will practice writing words with the difficult joinings of *b* and *o*.

Section Objectives

Review these objectives. When you have completed this section, you should be able to:

1. Explain how to select the main idea of an article, story, or a report.
6. Describe the power and the pattern of propaganda.
7. Explain the meaning of the word *internalize*.
8. Identify and use auxiliary verbs.
9. Identify and use verb phrases.
10. Form verb contractions.
15. Define and spell new words.
16. Practice handwriting skills.

Vocabulary

Study these words to enhance your learning success in this section.

editor (ed′ u tur). Person who has charge of a newspaper to decide what shall be printed in it.

editorial (ed u tôr′ ē ul). An article in a newspaper or magazine that gives the opinion or attitude of the paper on a certain subject.

internalize (in tėr′ nu līz). Applying information you read or learn to your own life.

personnel (pėr su nel′). Persons employed in any work, business, or service.

Pronunciation Key: hat, āge, cãre, fär; let, ēqual, tėrm; it, īce; hot, ōpen, ôrder; oil; out; cup, půt, rüle; child; long; thin; /ᴛʜ/ for then; /zh/ for measure; /u/ or /ə/ represents /a/ in about, /e/ in taken, /i/ in pencil, /o/ in lemon, and /u/ in circus.

RECOGNIZING PROPAGANDA

Propaganda is one of the powers of newspapers. Look for a pattern of propaganda as well as for the main ideas as you read the following selection.

PROPAGANDA: POWER AND PATTERN

One of the powers of newspapers is that of propaganda. Propaganda is a method used deliberately to influence people to believe certain ideas or to follow certain courses of action. On the **editorial** page the **editor** states personal ideas and beliefs about the issues of the times. Other pages contain news items the editor has chosen to print. Even in this selection, however, the editor may slant the news in favor of personal thoughts, using the power of propaganda.

Newspapers are not the only medium of propaganda. Posters, slogans, books, lectures, speeches, music, radio, television, the Internet, and all the people who write, print, produce, distribute, deliver, or direct these various media use propaganda.

A pattern of successful and effective propaganda has emerged through the years. This pattern includes organization, argument, persuasion, and publicity.

The first part of the pattern is organization. Propagandists choose the idea or products they want to sell, the attitudes of people they want to alter or change, the specialized **personnel** and tools they need, and the specific ideas and themes they must stress.

Appeals must be aimed at the creative thinkers as well as at the masses. Propaganda uses argument to appeal to a people's minds rather than their emotions. Claims must be sensible and not too far fetched. These arguments must be convincing to the intellectual person. Various methods, such as repeating certain words or ideas, may be used to convince the public.

When propagandists have converted the thinkers to their ideas, the task of leading the masses begins.

The next step of propaganda is persuasion or appealing to the emotions and senses. Propagandists may arouse favorable attitudes toward their causes, create fear of consequences for a different action, or play upon the desires and wants of the audience.

The last part of this pattern and probably the most important part is publicity. Propagandists must gain the attention of people so that their ideas, products, candidates, or causes can be spread. They have various channels of communication at their disposal. Almost any part of a newspaper can be used as a tool for propaganda—news stories, editorials, comics, cartoons, advertisements.

Propaganda may be positive or negative. Propagandists may be trying to convince people to brush their teeth regularly or to establish good eating habits. This type of propaganda is good.

Propaganda may be used to convince people to do or to buy something harmful or wrong. This type of propaganda is bad.

The reader or listener should consider several questions to see if the author is using good or bad propaganda.

1. What does the author want me to do or to buy?
2. What good will I receive from following the author's suggestions?
3. Why does the author want me to follow this suggestion: for their own good, for my good, or for the benefit of others?
4. Will I be going against any of my beliefs?

 Complete the following activities.

2.1 In a sentence write the main idea of "Propaganda: Power and Pattern."

_____

_____

2.2 List four parts of a pattern of propaganda.

a. _____   b. _____

c. _____   d. _____

2.3 Look through your local newspaper either a print copy or online.
List some ways your newspaper is trying to convince you to think or to buy something.

a. _____

_____

b. _____

_____

c. _____

_____

d. _____

_____

2.4 List four questions you should ask yourself about propaganda.

a. _____

_____

b. _____

_____

c. _____

_____

d. _____

_____

INTERNALIZING IDEAS

Often you may **internalize**, or apply to your own life, the information you read or learn.

In this section you have been studying propaganda. What have you learned about propaganda? Do you see propaganda used around you?

Do you buy things because of propaganda?

As you consider these questions you are internalizing. The following activity will give you another opportunity to internalize.

 Complete this activity.

2.5   Choose an advertisement about some product or an editorial about some issue.

    a. Decide if it uses positive or negative propaganda by asking yourself the four questions you listed in Activity 2.4.

    b. Write a paragraph explaining the decision you have made about this example of propaganda.

TEACHER CHECK _____ _____
                                   initials   date

LANGUAGE ARTS 608

LIFEPAC TEST

NAME _____

DATE _____

SCORE _____

LANGUAGE ARTS 608: LIFEPAC TEST

Answer true or false (each answer, 1 point).

1. _____ The main idea is the most important thing a writer wants you to know from their article or story.

2. _____ Fact is what has really happened.

3. _____ Opinion is what one thinks.

4. _____ A newspaper is a publication that tells happenings and information of general interest.

5. _____ Propaganda is a method deliberately used to influence thoughts or actions of people.

6. _____ An adverb functions as a predicate.

7. _____ A news story should always tell *when* and *where* a story happens.

8. _____ Censorship was established in the Bill of Rights.

9. _____ A verb is a word that shows action or being or linking.

10. _____ An adverb tells how, when, or where.

Place a slash mark / between the subject and predicate, and underline the verb (each part, 2 points).

11. Mayas carved events on monuments.

12. Alexander the Great sent news to Athens.

13. Newsletters were ancestors of newspapers.

14. Paper was made first in China.

Write the past tense of the verb in parentheses (each answer, 2 points).

15. (relay) African tribes _____ messages with drums.

16. (be) Sporting events _____ part of early newsletters.

17. (invent) Gutenberg _____ printing from movable type.

18. (contain) Early newspapers _____ only three or four pages.

19. (publish) Franklin _____ a paper in Pennsylvania.

Label the verb _v_ for action word, _be_ for form of be, _LV_ for linking verb (each answer, 2 points).

20.   Newspapers meet some human needs.

21.   Propaganda is a way of influencing people.

22.   Newsprint remains a major expense.

23.   Advertisements are one tool of propaganda.

Underline the auxiliary verb and circle the main verb in each sentence (each part, 2 points).

24.   Propaganda has influenced many people.

25.   Posters are enjoying popularity.

26.   Traveling may help reading.

27.   People will buy products from ads.

28.   Attitudes of people might change.

Match the words and contractions (each answer, 2 points).

29.   _____ haven't

30.   _____ isn't

31.   _____ won't

32.   _____ mustn't

33.   _____ shouldn't

34.   _____ don't

a.   should not

b.   do not

c.   must not

d.   is not

e.   have not

f.   will not

g.   were not

Underline the adverb or adverb phrase in each sentence (each answer, 2 points).

35.   Spring came early.

36.   It is raining slowly.

37.   Beautiful flowers are blooming in the garden.

38.   Our school is near the park.

39.   We play baseball during class.

Write the main idea of this paragraph (this answer, 5 points).

40. Newspapers are not the only medium of propaganda. Included are posters, slogans, pamphlets, books, sermons, speeches, Internet, radio, television—and all the people who write, print, produce, distribute, deliver, or direct these various media.

    _____

    _____

Complete these statements (each answer, 3 points).

41. An editor expresses their opinion by a. _____ and

    b. _____ .

42. A verb which does not form its tenses in the usual way is called _____ .

USING AUXILIARY VERBS

Auxiliary or helping verbs can be used to make some tenses. One important auxiliary verb is *be*. *Be* does not form tenses in the same way other verbs do. It is called *irregular* because you cannot always add *-s* or *-ed* to make present or past tense forms. *Be* follows no rules; you must memorize each form of *be*.

Study this verb.

Present		**Past**	
Singular	*Plural*	*Singular*	*Plural*
I *am*	we *are*	I *was*	we *were*
you *are*	you *are*	you *were*	you *were*
he, she, it *is*	they *are*	he, she, it *was*	they *were*

Examples: *I am* ready to go.
Karen *is* class president.
They *were* happy.
I *was* too excited to sleep.

 Write the correct form of *be* **on the line.**

2.6 I _____ at home now.

2.7 He _____ at school now.

2.8 We _____ at school yesterday.

2.9 You _____ my friend.

2.10 She _____ sick yesterday.

2.11 They _____ here now.

Other commonly used auxiliary verbs include *have, do, can, will, shall, may,* and *must*. Two of these verbs belong to the group of *irregular* verbs. Remember that irregular verbs do not form tenses by adding *-s* or *-ed*. The best way to form tenses in irregular verbs is by using a chart of principal parts or by using the dictionary.

Principal Parts of Verbs		
Present	**Past**	**Past Participle**
am (is, be)	was	been
do	did	done
have (has)	had	had

**Auxiliary
Verb**

Auxiliary verbs help certain forms of the main verb.

auxiliary	+	main verb	+	-ing	=	verb phrase
am	+	read	+	-ing	=	am reading
was	+	sing	+	-ing	=	was singing
are	+	go	+	-ing	=	are going

 Complete the following activity.

2.12 In these sentences circle the auxiliary verb and underline the main verb.

a. China was publishing papers before the invention of printing from movable type.

b. About ninety-seven out of every one hundred Americans have learned to read.

c. Almost every reader is reading the news online.

d. A newspaper in the home can exert a great deal of influence on the family.

e. A good editor does select newsworthy items.

f. A fair newspaper will present all sides of an issue.

g. A weekend edition may contain magazine sections and book reviews.

h. If printed in book form, a large newspaper would make a sizable volume.

i. If I am planning a career in journalism, I must learn English grammar.

A verb phrase is made up of the main verb used with one or more auxiliary verbs. Notice the verb phrases in the following example sentences.

He *can go*.

We *are running* to town.

Can you *see* that star?

 Complete the following activities.

2.13 In these sentences underline the verb phrases.

a. Rebekah had been told by the Lord, "Two sons shall be born to you."

b. "The older will serve the younger."

c. At birth Jacob was holding Esau's heel.

d. Esau had hunted game while Jacob was cooking lentil stew.

e. Esau would have been given Isaac's blessing if he had not sold his birthright.

2.14 Write sentences using these main verbs with one or more auxiliary verbs.

a. sing _____

_____

b. pray _____

_____

c. preach _____

_____

d. give _____

_____

TEACHER CHECK _____ _____

initials   date

The word *not* can be added to any of the
helping verbs: *is not, were not, has not, did not,
cannot, would not.*

These words can be written shorter as
contractions. In place of *o* write an apostrophe
('): *isn't, weren't, hasn't, didn't, can't, wouldn't.*
You will notice that the contraction is one word.

 Complete the following activities.

2.15 Write the contractions for these words.

a. cannot _____   e. do not _____

b. did not _____   f. was not _____

c. have not _____   g. had not _____

d. are not _____   h. would not _____

2.16 Write the words for these contractions.

a. doesn't _____   e. isn't _____

b. won't _____   f. hasn't _____

c. weren't _____   g. shouldn't _____

d. couldn't _____   h. aren't _____

TEACHER CHECK _____ _____
                                initials   date

SPELLING AND HANDWRITING

In this section you will study some new words and practice the letters *b* and *o*.

Spelling. Learn the meanings and spellings of the words in Spelling Words-2. You will recognize
words about propaganda as well as science terms in this list.

SPELLING WORDS-2

propaganda	publicity	hypothesis
influence	atmosphere	infection
pattern	capillary	nucleus
emerge	carbohydrate	observation
conviction	digestion	organism
effective	ecology	parasite
organization	fossil	predict
argument	galaxy	pulse
persuasion		

 Complete the following activities.

2.17 In your best handwriting arrange the spelling list in alphabetical order.

Draw a line between syllables. You may find help in your dictionary.

a. _____   b. _____

c. _____   d. _____

e. _____   f. _____

g. _____   h. _____

i. _____   j. _____

k. _____   l. _____

m. _____   n. _____

o. _____   p. _____

q. _____   r. _____

s. _____   t. _____

u. _____   v. _____

w. _____   x. _____

y. _____

2.18 List the ten words that refer to propaganda.

a. _____   b. _____

c. _____   d. _____

e. _____   f. _____

g. _____   h. _____

i. _____   j. _____

2.19 Write the meanings of these science terms. Use your dictionary.

a. atmosphere _____

_____

b. capillary _____

_____

c. carbohydrate _____

_____

d. digestion _____

_____

e. ecology _____

_____

f. fossil _____

_____

g. galaxy _____

_____

h. hypothesis _____

_____

i. infection _____

_____

j. nucleus _____

_____

k. observation _____

_____

l. organism _____

_____

m. parasite _____

_____

n. predict _____

_____

o. pulse _____

_____

2.20 Ask a fellow student to study the spelling words with you.

TEACHER CHECK _____ _____

initials   date

ABC **Ask your teacher to give you a practice spelling test of Spelling Words-2.** Restudy the words you missed.

Handwriting. Be sure to form the entire *b* before writing the next letter. Remember that the flag on *o* is in the air.

Examples: Do not write ⓑ , write ⓑ .

Do not write ⓞ , write ⓞ .

🖉   **Complete the following handwriting activities.**

2.21 Write a line of each letter.

b

o

2.22 Write one line of each of the following words.

board

book

bobbin

bobolink

above

object

oblique

blow

oboe

bowl

Review the material in this section to prepare for the Self Test. This Self Test will check your understanding of this section and will review the first section. Any items you miss in the following test will show you what areas you need to restudy.

SELF TEST 2

Match the following items (each answer, 2 points).

2.01 _____ propaganda

2.02 _____ media

2.03 _____ auxiliary

2.04 _____ censorship

2.05 _____ editorial

a. act of making news reports satisfactory to a government or an organization

b. news articles giving the editor's opinion

c. all copies of a book or newspaper printed alike and at the same time

d. a plan or method used to spread beliefs or opinions

e. a helper

f. a means of communicating thoughts, ideas, or opinions

Write the past tense of the word in parentheses (each answer, 2 points).

2.06 (be) February 12, 1809, _____ Lincoln's birthday.

2.07 (study) He _____ law with a friend.

2.08 (be) He _____ President of the United States.

2.09 (pray) George Washington _____ at Valley Forge.

2.010 (serve) He _____ his country well.

Put a slash mark / between the subject and predicate and underline the verb phrase (each part, 2 points).

2.011 The groundhog did not see his shadow.

2.012 Valentine's Day will come again next year.

2.013 Did you send cards to your friends?

2.014 Mr. Lincoln might have remained a country lawyer.

2.015 His Gettysburg Address is being memorized by many young people.

2.016 Mr. Booth may have been killed the same night of Mr. Lincoln's death.

Write the contraction for the words in parentheses (each answer, 2 points).

2.017 _____ Washington (did not) cross the Amazon River.

2.018 _____ He (was not) a military man by profession.

2.019 _____ At Valley Forge his men (were not) fed properly.

2.020 _____ He (would not) be president again.

2.021 _____ Mt. Vernon (is not) closed to the American people.

Complete the following statements (each blank, 3 points).

2.022 The three degrees of comparison in adjectives are a. _____ ,

b. _____ , and c. _____ .

2.023 The four steps, or parts, of a pattern of propaganda are

a. _____ , b. _____ , c. _____ , and

d. _____ .

2.024 Three media of propaganda are a. _____ , b. _____ , and

c. _____ .

2.025 When you apply information to your own life, you _____ .

2.026 When a verb cannot form its tenses by adding -*ed*, it is called _____ .

2.027 Three auxiliary verbs are a. _____ , b. _____ , and

c. _____ .

2.028 The present, past, and past participle forms of a verb are called _____ .

Answer true or false (each answer, 1 point).

2.029 _____ An editorial is an article telling news.

2.030 _____ An editorial is used to explain the editor's opinion.

2.031 _____ Propaganda can be good or bad.

2.032 _____ The Bill of Rights is the same as the first ten amendments.

2.033 _____ A verb always shows action.

Answer the following question (this answer, 5 points).

2.034 How can you tell if propaganda is positive or negative?

_____

_____

_____

_____

_____

```
 80
/
100
```
SCORE _____ **TEACHER** _____ _____
                                              initials   date

ABC
Take your spelling test of Spelling Words-2.

3. SECTION THREE

In this section you will analyze a news story, studying the parts composing it. Then you will write a news article of your own.

You will learn more about one word adverbs and study about adverb phrases. You will study spelling and handwriting skills. Your spelling list will include adverbs and more science terms. In handwriting you will practice writing sentences with words using the letters *w, v, b,* and *o.*

Section Objectives

Review these objectives. When you have finished this section, you should be able to:

11. List the parts of a news story.

12. Explain how to analyze a news story.

13. Identify and use adverbs.

14. Identify and use adverb phrases.

15. Define and spell new words.

16. Practice handwriting skills.

Vocabulary

Study these words to enhance your learning success in this section.

analyze (an' u līz). Examine carefully to separate the elements of anything.

by-line (bī' līn). Line at the beginning of a newspaper or magazine article giving the name of the writer.

headline (hed' līn). Words printed in heavy type at the top of a newspaper article describing the content.

Pronunciation Key: hat, āge, cãre, fär; let, ēqual, tėrm; it, īce; hot, ōpen, ôrder; oil; out; cup, půt, rüle; child; long; thin; /ŦH/ for then; /zh/ for measure; /u/ or /ə/ represents /a/ in about, /e/ in taken, /i/ in pencil, /o/ in lemon, and /u/ in circus.

ANALYZING A NEWS STORY

A news story is written so that the most import-ant ideas come first. Sometimes the first para-graph of a news story contains all the main ideas. The next paragraph gives more informa-tion about the first paragraph. The following paragraphs give details about the story.

Because the last paragraph or two of a news story provides details, the story can be easily shortened if needed.

All news stories should answer six important questions.

When you **analyze** a news story, you should find answers to the following questions:

What has happened?

Who did the action?

When did it happen?

Where did it happen?

How did it happen?

Why did it happen?

A news story can be analyzed in almost the same way a story can be analyzed. The *setting* of a story explains *where* and *when* the action takes place. The *characters* are those people who take part in the story. The *plot* describes *what* happened. It is the main order of action in a story. A story often explains *how* and *why* the action takes place.

DENTAL HEALTH FAIR TO FOCUS ON CHILDREN

The Central Arizona and East Valley Dental Hygienists' Societies will provide free dental inspections for children 12 years and under at the third annual Children's Dental Health Fair set for this weekend.

The fair is scheduled from 10 a.m. to 5 p.m. at Park Central Shopping Center, Phoenix.

Children 12 and under accompanied by a parent will be receiving free toothbrushes and instruction on brushing, as well as the dental inspection by a dentist.

There will also be a consumer information booth and nutrition booth offering help and advice to parents and continuous entertainment, with a dental message, throughout the day – including, the "Tooth Fairy Show" starring the Tooth Fairy and Yukky Plaque, free movies, balloons and drawings.

In the news story you just read from the *Tempe Daily News* (Tempe, Arizona) the **headline** states the main idea in the story. The first paragraph tells *who, what, where* and *when* the story takes place. If this story had been signed by the reporter who wrote it, a **by-line** would appear under the headlines.

Complete the following activities.

3.1 Explain the order in which a news story is written.

_____

_____

_____

3.2 List the six questions a good news story should answer.

a. _____   b. _____

c. _____   d. _____

e. _____   f. _____

Match the following terms.

3.3 _____ headline

3.4 _____ by-line

3.5 _____ when and where

3.6 _____ who

3.7 _____ analyze

a. line above a story telling the author

b. like the characters in a story

c. carefully examine the elements of some-thing where

d. the name of the newspaper

e. like the setting of a story

f. printed in heavy type above the story

g. internalize

Complete the following activities.

3.8 Select a news story from your local newspaper. Then complete the following analysis.

a. headline _____

b. by-line _____

c. setting (when and where?) _____

d. characters (who?) _____

e. plot (what?) _____

_____

f. how? _____

g. why? _____

3.9 Now *you* write a news item on a separate piece of paper. Perhaps an interesting event happened at school, at home, or in your town. If you analyze it here, it probably will be easier to write as a news story.

a. headline _____

   by-line _____

   setting _____

   characters _____

   _____

   plot _____

   _____

   _____

   how? _____

   _____

   _____

   why? _____

   _____

TEACHER CHECK _____ _____
                    initials   date

b. Share your news story with a friend.

TEACHER CHECK _____ _____
                    initials   date

USING ADVERBS

An adverb is a word that modifies, or changes, an action verb. It tells *when, where,* or *how* something happened. The following sentences contain adverbs:

1. I will finish *later*. *When* will I finish? Later.

2. Hang your coat *there*. *Where* should you hang it? There.

3. Ellen ran *quickly* to the telephone. *How* did she run? Quickly.

An adverb may be one word or it may be more than one word. Several words can also be used together to modify a verb. An adverb of more than one word is called an adverb phrase. Even though a phrase may have another name, it is called an adverb phrase when it is used as an adverb.

Look at the following sentences.

	Adverbs	Phrases used as adverbs
Where?	Wait *there*.	Wait *in the garden*.
When?	I'll see you *later*.	I'll see you *after dinner*.
How?	Jan sang *happily*.	Jan sang with *great happiness*.

These examples show that adverb phrases act in the same way that adverbs do.

 Circle the adverbs and adverb phrases in the following sentences.

3.10 Can you come here?

3.11 I will see you after school.

3.12 Drive with care.

The phrases used in the examples and activities are also called prepositional phrases, but they are used as adverbs. Not all prepositional phrases are used as adverbs.

You may remember that a prepositional phrase is a preposition followed by a noun or a pronoun. Look at the prepositions in the following list.

about	below	for	over
above	beneath	from	through
against	beside	in	to
among	between	into	toward
around	beyond	near	under
at	by	of	with
before	down	off	within
behind	during	on	without

Some of the prepositions have been made into prepositional phrases in the following list.

above the clouds	during class
among us	from God
at home	in the store
beside them	near the boys
by the stream	over the bridge

Remember when a prepositional phrase tells *when, where,* or *how,* it is used as an *adverb phrase.*

 Write an adverb phrase in place of the adverb in the following sentences.

3.13 The car moved (speedily) _____ down the road.

3.14 The man answered (angrily) _____.

3.15 I will be home (early) _____.

3.16 Wait for me (there) _____.

3.17 I will see you (then) _____.

3.18 Can you come (quietly) _____?

Put a slash mark / between the subject and predicate. Label the verb *v* for action verb, *be* for a form of be, and *LV* for linking verb. Underline the adverb or adverb phrase and circle the preposition.

3.19 Newspapers come daily.

3.20 Publishers print from movable type.

3.21 Some newspapers remain in one family.

3.22 Propaganda seems false sometimes.

3.23 Moses heard God through the burning bush.

3.24 Samuel listened to God's voice.

3.25 Elijah prayed at Mt. Carmel.

3.26 The angel choir sang at Jesus' birth.

3.27 Paul preached on Mars Hill.

3.28 John saw a vision on Patmos.

TEACHER CHECK _____ _____
                    initials   date

SPELLING AND HANDWRITING

You will learn to spell some newspaper and science terms in this spelling list. You will practice joining the letters *w, v, b,* and *o* to other letters.

Spelling. Learn the meaning and spelling of each word in Spelling Words-3.

SPELLING WORDS-3

earliest	dermis	stethoscope
by-line	eclipse	tendon
headline	mammal	tissue
analyze	recycle	universe
editor	rust	vertebrate
opinion	saliva	X-ray
scoop	science	yeast
cell	skeleton	

Complete the following activities.

3.29 In your best handwriting arrange the spelling words in alphabetical order.
Draw a line between the syllables. Use your dictionary.

a. _____   b. _____

c. _____   d. _____

e. _____   f. _____

g. _____   h. _____

i. _____   j. _____

k. _____   l. _____

m. _____   n. _____

o. _____   p. _____

q. _____   r. _____

s. _____   t. _____

u. _____   v. _____

w. _____

3.30 Write sentences with words that refer to newspapers. Be sure your meanings are correct.

a. _____

b. _____

c. _____

d. _____

e. _____

f. _____

3.31 List the words that are science terms.

a. _____   b. _____

c. _____   d. _____

e. _____   f. _____

g. _____   h. _____

i. _____   j. _____

k. _____   l. _____

m. _____   n. _____

o. _____   p. _____

ABC   **Ask your teacher to give you a practice spelling test of Spelling Words-3.** Restudy the words you missed.

Handwriting. Be careful as you join *w, v, b,* and *o* to other letters.

3.32 Write each sentence two times.

News sources meet valuable needs.

Propaganda observes few rules.

Adverbs tell when, where, and how.

Before taking the last Self Test, you may want to do one or more of these self checks.

1. _____ Read the objectives. See if you can do them.
2. _____ Restudy the material related to any objectives that you cannot do.
3. _____ Use the **SQ3R** study procedure to review the material.
   a. **S**can the sections.
   b. **Q**uestion yourself.
   c. **R**ead to answer your questions.
   d. **R**ecite the answers to yourself.
   e. **R**eview areas you did not understand.
4. _____ Review all vocabulary, activities, and Self Tests, writing a correct answer for every wrong answer.

SELF TEST 3

Write the definitions of the following terms (each answer, 4 points).

3.01 newspaper _____

_____

3.02 propaganda _____

_____

3.03 editor _____

_____

3.04 by-line _____

_____

3.05 fact _____

_____

3.06 opinion _____

_____

3.07 auxiliary _____

_____

3.08 censorship _____

_____

3.09 media _____

_____

Complete the following sentences (each answer, 3 points).

3.010 Adverbs tell a. _____ , b. _____ , and

c. _____ .

3.011 A prepositional phrase used as an adverb is called an _____ .

Place a slash mark / between the subject and the predicate and underline the adverb or adverb phrase (each part, 2 points).

3.012   Spring will come soon.

3.013   We planted seeds in the garden.

3.014   It rained slowly.

3.015   Flowers are blooming now.

3.016   Crops will grow later.

3.017   The birds can eat from the plowed fields.

3.018   We shall harvest by June.

3.019   We shall eat bountifully.

3.020   We are truly grateful.

Complete the following activities (each part, 2 points).

3.021 Write a contraction for these words.

a. cannot _____

b. would not _____

3.022 Write the comparative and superlative degrees for these words.

a. big, _____ , _____

b. cold, _____ , _____

3.023 Write a one-word adverb for each adverb phrase.

a. in the garden _____

b. after lunch _____

80/100 SCORE _____ TEACHER _____ _____
initials   date

ABC

Take your spelling test of Spelling Words-3.

Before taking the LIFEPAC Test, you may want to do one or more of these self checks.

1. _____ Read the objectives. See if you can do them.
2. _____ Restudy the material related to any objectives that you cannot do.
3. _____ Use the **SQ3R** study procedure to review the material.
4. _____ Review activities, Self Tests, and LIFEPAC vocabulary words.
5. _____ Restudy areas of weakness indicated by the last Self Test.
6. _____ Review all Spelling Words in this LIFEPAC.